初級日本語

〔げんき〕

AN INTEGRATED COURSE IN
ELEMENTARY JAPANESE

GENKI

SECOND EDITION

げんき

〔第2版〕

I

ワークブック

WORKBOOK

Eri Banno　坂野永理

Yoko Ikeda　池田庸子

Yutaka Ohno　大野裕

Chikako Shinagawa　品川恭子

Kyoko Tokashiki　渡嘉敷恭子

The Japan Times

付属ディスクについて
付属のディスクには、MP3 形式のデジタル音声ファイルが収録されています。
コンピューターやデジタルオーディオ機器で再生してください。
CD プレーヤーでは再生できませんので、ご注意ください。

Note on the accompanying disk
The disk that comes with this book contains digital audio files in MP3 format.
The files can be played on computers or digital audio players, but not on CD players.

First edition: February 2000
Second edition: March 2011
25th printing: March 2015

Illustrations: Noriko Udagawa
English translations and copyreading: 4M Associates, Inc., and Umes Corp.
Narrators: Miho Nagahori, Yumiko Muro, Tomoki Kusumi, Tsuyoshi Yokoyama,
          and Kit Pancoast Nagamura
Recordings: TBS Service, Inc.
Typesetting: guild
Cover art and editorial design: Nakayama Design Office
                    Gin-o Nakayama and Akihito Kaneko
Printing: Tosho Printing Co., Ltd.

Published by The Japan Times, Ltd.
5-4, Shibaura 4-chome, Minato-ku, Tokyo 108-0023, Japan
Phone: 03-3453-2013
Website: http://bookclub.japantimes.co.jp/
Genki-Online: http://genki.japantimes.co.jp/

ISBN4-7890-1441-0

Printed in Japan

本書について

　このワークブックはテキスト『初級日本語 げんき』の補助教材です。今回『げんき』を改訂するにあたり、テキストの改訂内容に合わせてワークブックも加筆修正を行いました。そして、従来からあった文法練習、聞く練習、漢字の練習に加えて、「答えましょう」を各課に追加しました。この練習には、その課の学習項目を使って自由に答える質問が載っており、会話練習や復習として使えます。また、「聞く練習」の音声を MP3 ファイルにして本書に添付し、より使いやすくしました。

　本書の「会話・文法編」には、テキストで導入された各文法項目につき1ページのワークシートがあります。ワークシートでは既習の文法項目や語彙も復習しながら学習項目の定着を図ることができます。

　各文法項目を学習した後は、「聞く練習」と「答えましょう」で総合的な練習を行うことができます。「聞く練習」には1課につき、会話文を中心として3つまたは4つの問題が収録してあります。

　「読み書き編」は、漢字の練習シート（Kanji Practice）と漢字の穴埋め問題（Using Kanji）で構成されています。『げんきⅠ』のワークブックには英文和訳もあります。漢字の導入後、書き方を覚えるまで、この漢字練習シートを使って何度も書いてみましょう。まず、漢字のバランスを意識して薄く書かれている文字をなぞってから、右側の空欄に何度も書いて練習します。筆順はテキストの漢字表を参考にしてください。

　穴埋め問題は、文の中に漢字や熟語が意味のあるものとして含まれていますから、必ず文全体を読んでから解答してください。『げんきⅠ』の英文和訳の練習では、習った漢字をできるだけ使って文を書いてみましょう。

　テキストとこのワークブックを併用することで、より効率よく初級日本語を学ぶことができるでしょう。

About This Book

This workbook is designed as a supplement for the textbook *GENKI: An Integrated Course in Elementary Japanese*. Revisions made in the second edition have required additions and other changes to the workbook to bring it into conformity with the new text. In addition to the grammar, listening and kanji drills that were a part of the old workbook, we've added a Questions section to each chapter, which allows students to create answers freely, using what they have learned in that chapter. Finally, the addition of MP3 format audio aids to the Listening Comprehension sections has made the workbook easier to use.

The Conversation and Grammar section in this book contains a worksheet for each grammar point introduced in the textbook. In addition to providing practice on new material, the worksheets also help students to reinforce their understanding of grammatical topics and vocabulary encountered in earlier lessons.

After studying each new grammatical idea, students are given the opportunity to review the material comprehensively through the Listening Comprehension and Questions sections. The Listening Comprehension section for each lesson features three or four tasks that involve listening to dialogues and other recorded material.

The Reading and Writing section consists of kanji worksheets (Kanji Practice) and fill-in-the-blank questions about the kanji (Using Kanji). (Volume 1 also includes English-to-Japanese translations.) Newly introduced kanji should be written over and over on the sheet until memorized. First, trace the lightly printed kanji samples, paying attention to the balance of the characters. Then practice by copying the kanji over and over again in the blank spaces to the right. For stroke order, please refer to the kanji chart in the textbook.

For the fill-in-the-blank questions, students should read the entire sentence before filling in the blanks in order to learn kanji in context. When practicing the English-to-Japanese translations in Volume 1, students should use previously studied kanji whenever possible.

By using this workbook in tandem with the textbook, students will learn elementary Japanese with greater efficiency.

げんき①ワークブック　もくじ

会話・文法編
かい　　わ　　ぶん　ぽう　　へん
Conversation and Grammar Section

あいさつ ■ Greetings

▶ What are these people saying? Write in Japanese (*hiragana*) the appropriate expression for each situation.

1. <u>おはよう</u>

2. <u>ありがとう</u>

が _g

3. <u>こんばんは</u>
    は

4. <u>すみません</u>
   すみません

5. <u>いただきます</u>
  いただきます

6. <u>ごちそうさま（でした）</u>
  ごちそうさま（でした）

7. <u>いってきます</u>

8. <u>いってらっしゃい</u>

9. <u>ただいま</u>

10. <u>おかえりなさい</u>

11. <u>はじめまして</u>

12. <u>さようなら</u>

13. <u>おやすみなさい</u>

14. <u>こんにちは</u>

第1課 1 Numbers
だい いっ か

▶ Write the following numbers in Arabic numerals.

(1) ご _____5_____

(2) ぜろ _____0_____

(3) きゅう _____9_____

(4) さん _____3_____

(5) なな _____7_____

(6) に _____2_____

(7) ろく _____6_____

(8) いち _____1_____

(9) はち _____8_____

(10) よん _____4_____

(11) じゅうろく _____16_____

(12) よんじゅう _____40_____

(13) にじゅういち _____21_____

(14) ひゃくろくじゅうよん _____164_____

(15) きゅうじゅうに _____92_____

(16) さんじゅうご _____35_____

(17) ななじゅうろく _____76_____

(18) じゅうはち _____18_____

(19) ひゃくごじゅうなな _____157_____

(20) ひゃくいち _____101_____

zero ぜろ = 0   なな = 7
ichi いち = 1   はち = 8
ni に = 2   きゅう = 9
san さん = 3   じゅう = 10
yon よん = 4
go ご = 5
roku ろく = 6

第1課 2 Time and Telephone Numbers
だい いっ か

(I) Time—Look at the following pictures and write the answers.

1. **05:00** PM
   Q：いま なんじですか。
   A：ごごごじ です

2. **09:00** AM
   Q：いま なんじですか。
   A：ごぜん きゅじです

3. **12:30** PM
   Q：いま なんじですか。
   A：ごご じゅうにじ はん です

4. **04:30** AM
   Q：いま なんじですか。
   A：ごぜん よんじ はん です

(II) Telephone Numbers—Ask three people what their phone numbers are and write down the numbers in both Japanese and Arabic numerals.

1. _____
   (Arabic numerals: 　　　　　　　　　　)

2. _____
   (Arabic numerals: 　　　　　　　　　　)

3. _____
   (Arabic numerals: 　　　　　　　　　　)

第1課 3 Noun₁ の Noun₂・X は Y です
だい いっ か

(I) Translate the following phrases into Japanese using the framework "AのB." Note carefully that the order in which the two nouns appear may be different in English and in Japanese. Read Grammar 3 (pp. 44-45).

1. Japanese student　にほんご の がくせい

2. Takeshi's telephone number　たけし さん の でんわ ばんご

3. my friend　わたし の ともたち

4. English-language teacher　えいご の せんせい

5. Michiko's major　みちこ の せんこう

(II) Using the framework "X は Y です," translate the following sentences into Japanese.

1. Ms. Ogawa is Japanese.
おがや さん　は　にほん人　です。

2. Mr. Takeda is a teacher.
たけだ さん は せんせい です

3. I am an international student.
りゅうがくせい です

4. Haruna is a first-year student.
はるな は いちねんせい です

5. Ms. Yamamoto is 25 years old.
やまもと さん は にじゅうご さい です

6. My major is Japanese.
せんこう は にほんじん です

第1課 4 Question Sentences
だい いっ か

(Ⅰ) Ask the right questions in each of the following exchanges.

1. You : なん ねんせい ですか

   Kimura : よねんせいです。

2. You : せんこうは なん ですか

   Kimura : れきしです。

3. You : きむら は なんさい ですか

   Kimura : じゅうきゅうさいです。

4. You : でんわ ばんごう は なん ですか

   Kimura : よんさんの ろくきゅういちななです。

5. You : すみません。いま なんじ ですか

   Kimura : いま くじはんです。

(Ⅱ) Translate the following sentences into Japanese.

1. Are you a student?

   がくせい ですか

   Yes, I am a student at Nihon University.

   はい。わたし は にほん だいがく の がくせい です

2. Is Michiko a fourth-year student?

   みちこ は よねんせい ですか

   No, Michiko is a third-year student.

   いいえ。みちこ は さんねんせい です

第1課 5 きくれんしゅう (Listening Comprehension)
だい いっ か

Ⓐ Listen to the phrases and choose the correct picture from below. 📢 W01-A

1. (h)   2. (k)   3. (g)   4. (a)   5. (e)   6. (j)

7. (f)   8. (c)   9. (b)   10. (i)   11. (d)

しち

B Listen to the dialogues between a passenger and a flight attendant in an airplane. Find out the times of the following cities. 🔊 W01-B

Example:　とうきょう ___8:00 A.M.___

1. パリ (Paris)　　　~~LAK~~ 4 PM
2. ソウル (Seoul)　　~~7PM~~ 9PM
3. ニューヨーク (New York)　1PM
4. ロンドン (London)　7:30 ~~PM~~ AM
5. タイペイ (Taipei)　11 AM
6. シドニー (Sydney)　3:30 PM

C Listen to the dialogues between Mr. Tanaka and a telephone operator. Find out the telephone numbers of the following people. 🔊 W01-C

Example:　すずき ___51-6751___

1. かわさき　905-0877
2. リー (Lee)　5934-1026
3. ウッズ (Woods)　49-1509
4. トンプソン (Thompson)　6782-3333

D Two students, Akira and Kate, are talking. Mark ○ if the following statements are true. Mark ✕ if not true. 🔊 W01-D

1. (○) Akira is a first-year student.
2. (✕) Akira is a student at the University of America.
3. (✕) Akira's major is history.
4. (✕) Kate is a second-year student.
5. (○) Kate's major is Japanese.

第1課 6 こたえましょう (Questions)
だい いっ か

▶ Answer the following questions in Japanese.

1. おなまえは？

はらど です

2. しごと (occupation) は なんですか。

かいしゃいん です

3. なんねんせいですか。

いえ。わたし は がくせい じゃない です

4. なんさいですか。

さんじゅう さい です

5. せんこうは なんですか。

かがく です

6. でんわばんごうは なんですか。

しし きゅ の ご きゅ に きゅ

第2課 だい に か 1 Numbers

（Ⅰ）Write the following numbers in Arabic numerals.

(1) よんひゃくななじゅう　470

(2) はっぴゃく ごじゅう さん　853
800　　50　　3

(3) せんさんびゃく　1300
1000　300

(4) いちまんななせん　17,000
10,000　7,000

(5) さんぜんろっぴゃくじゅうに　3612
3000　600　12

(6) ごせんひゃくきゅうじゅうはち　5198
5000　100　98

(7) よんまんろくせんきゅうひゃく　36,900
30,000　6,000　900

(8) きゅうまんにひゃくじゅう　90,210
90,000　200　10

（Ⅱ）Write the following numbers in *hiragana*.

1. 541　　ごひゃく よんじゅう いち

2. 2,736　　にせん なな ひゃく さんじゅう ろく

3. 8,900　　はっせん きゅひゃく

4. 12,345　　いちまん にせん さんびゃく よじゅうご

（Ⅲ）Look at the pictures and complete the dialogues.

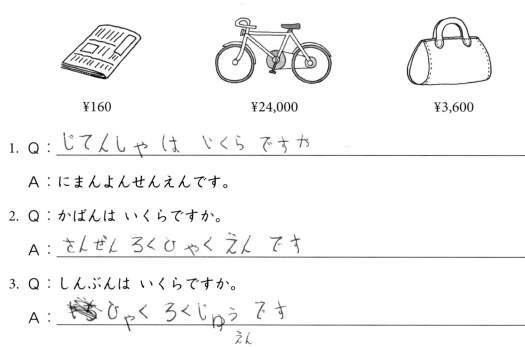

¥160　　　　　　¥24,000　　　　　　¥3,600

1. Q：じてんしゃ は いくら ですか

　　A：にまんよんせんえんです。

2. Q：かばんは いくらですか。

　　A：さんぜん ろくひゃく えん です

3. Q：しんぶんは いくらですか。

　　A：ひゃく ろくじゅう です
　　　　　　　　　　えん

第2課 2 これ, それ, and あれ
だい に か

(Ⅰ) Look at the pictures and translate the sentences into Japanese.

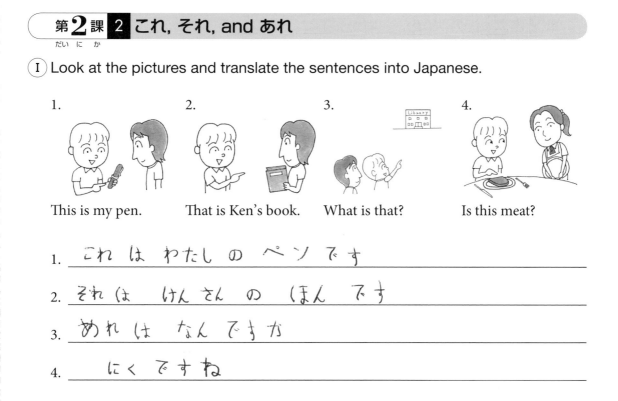

1.   This is my pen.   2.   That is Ken's book.   3.   What is that?   4.   Is this meat?

1. これ は わたし の ペン です

2. それ は けん さん の ほん です

3. あれ は なん ですか

4. にく です ね

(Ⅱ) Mary and Takeshi are talking. Look at the picture and fill in これ, それ, or あれ.

メアリー : 1. これ は たけしさんの かさですか。
めありい

たけし : いいえ、2. それ は みちこさんの かさです。

3. これ は メアリーさんの さいふですか。
めありい

メアリー : ええ、わたしの さいふです。
めありい

たけしさん、4. あれ は たけしさんの じてんしゃですか。

たけし : ええ、そうです。

メアリー : 5. あれ は なんですか。
めありい

たけし : ゆうびんきょくです。

第2課 3 この, その, and あの
だい に か

▶ Complete the following conversation between the attendant and the customer at a watch shop.

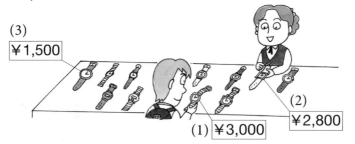

(3) ¥1,500

(1) ¥3,000

(2) ¥2,800

Attendant:　いらっしゃいませ。

Customer (*pointing at watch #1*):　1. この とけい は ~~いくら~~ いくら ですか 。
(How much is this watch?)

Attendant:　そのとけいは さんぜんえんです。

Customer (*pointing at watch #2*):　2. その とけい は いくら ですか 。
(How much is that watch?)

Attendant:　3. この とけい は にせん はっぴゃく えんです 。

Customer (*pointing at watch #3*):　4. あの とけい は いくら ですか 。
(How much is that watch?)

Attendant:　5. あの とけい は いちせん ~~~~ ごひゃく えん です 。

Customer (*decided on #3*):　6. じゃあ あの とけい をください 。
(Then, I'll take that watch.)

第2課 4 ここ, そこ, and あそこ・だれの
だい に か

Ⅰ You are B. Answer A's questions with ここ, そこ, or あそこ.

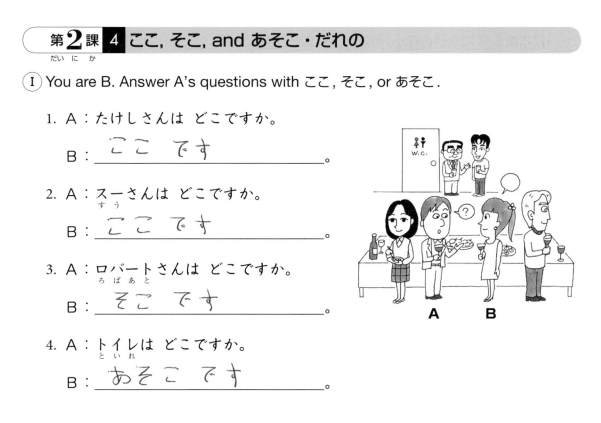

1. A：たけしさんは　どこですか。

   B：＿ここ　です＿＿＿＿＿＿＿＿。

2. A：スーさんは　どこですか。
   すう

   B：＿ここ　です＿＿＿＿＿＿＿＿。

3. A：ロバートさんは　どこですか。
   ろ ば あ と

   B：＿そこ　です＿＿＿＿＿＿＿＿。

4. A：トイレは　どこですか。
   と い れ

   B：＿あそこ　です＿＿＿＿＿＿＿。

Ⅱ Your friends left their belongings in your room. Ask Michiko whose items these are.

1. You：＿これ は だれ の ぼうしですか＿＿。

   みちこ：それは　たけしさんの　ぼうしです。

2. You：＿これ は だれ の さいふ です か＿。

   みちこ：それは　わたしの　さいふです。

3. You：＿これ は だれ の かさ です か＿＿。

   みちこ：あれは　メアリーさんの　かさです。
   め あ り い

第2課 5 Noun も・Noun じゃないです
だい に か

(I) Translate the following sentences into Japanese. Use も after the underscored phrases.

1. Ms. Tanaka is Japanese. <u>Mr. Yoshida</u> is Japanese, too.

たなか さん は にほん人 です. よしだ さん も にほん人 です

2. Ms. Tanaka is twenty years old. <u>Mr. Yoshida</u> is twenty years old, too.

たなか さん は にじゅうさい です. よしだ さん も にじゅうさい です

3. This dictionary is 2,000 yen. <u>That dictionary</u> is 2,000 yen, too.

このじしょ は にせん えん です. そのじしょ も にせん えん です

4. This is my bicycle. <u>That</u> is my bicycle, too.

これは
わたしの ~~これは~~ じてんしゃ です. ~~それは~~ これ ~~は~~ も わたし の じてんしゃ です

5. Takeshi's major is history. <u>My major</u> is history, too.

~~たかしの せんこう~~
~~たかし~~ の せんこう は れきし です. わたし の せんこう ~~は~~ も れきし です

(II) Answer the following questions in the negative. These are all personal questions. "○○" (read まるまる) stands for your name. You will want to replace it with わたし in your answers.

1. ○○さんは かいしゃいん (office worker) ですか。

~~わたしさん は~~ かいしゃいん じゃ ない です

2. ○○さんは にほんじんですか。

いいえ. も じゃない ですよ

3. ○○さんの せんこうは れきしですか。

わたし の せんこう は れきし じゃない です

4. あれは ○○さんの じてんしゃですか。

あれは わたしの じてんしゃ じゃない です

5. それは ○○さんの かさですか。

それは わたしの かさ じゃない です

第2課 だいにか 6 きくれんしゅう (Listening Comprehension)

Ⓐ Listen to the dialogue at a kiosk and find out the prices of the following items. If you can't find out the price, indicate such with a question mark (?). W02-A

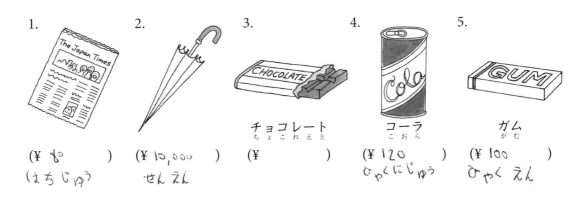

1.　2.　3.　4.　5.

チョコレート
ちょこれえと

コーラ
こおら

ガム
がむ

(¥ 80　)　(¥ 10,000　)　(¥　　)　(¥ 120　)　(¥ 100　)
はちじゅう　　せんえん　　　　　　　ひゃくにじゅう　　ひゃくえん

Ⓑ Mary introduces her friend, Christy, to Takeshi. Answer the following questions in Japanese. W02-B　　　＊フランス (France)
ふらんす

1. クリスティさんは アメリカじんですか。
くりすてぃ　　あめりか
　　いいえ アメリカ人 じゃ ない です

2. クリスティさんの せんこうは なんですか。
くりすてぃ
　　えいご です

3. クリスティさんの おとうさんは にほんじんですか。
くりすてぃ
　　ええ そうです

4. クリスティさんの おかあさんは にほんじんですか。
くりすてぃ
　　いいえ ふらんす人 です

Ⓒ Mary and Takeshi went to a Japanese restaurant. They are looking at the menu. W02-C

1. How much are these items?

　a. すきやき (¥3,000　) b. うどん (¥ 600　) c. てんぷら (¥ 1100　)
　　(pot)　　　　　　　(noodle)　　　　　　　(deep fry)

2. Mark ◯ if the following statements are true. Mark ✕ if not true.

　a. (✕) *Sukiyaki* has fish in it.

　b. (◯) Mary thinks *sukiyaki* is expensive.

　c. (◯) Both Takeshi and Mary ordered *udon*.

第2課 7 こたえましょう (Questions)
だい に か

▶ Answer the following questions in Japanese.

1. にほんじんですか。

いいえ。じゃないです

2. にねんせいですか。

いいえ。~~さん~~ よねんせい です

3. せんこうは けいざいですか。

いいえ けいざい じゃ ない です

4. おかあさんは にほんじんですか。

いいえ　アメリカ人 です

5. おとうさんは なんさいですか。

ろくじゅうさい です

6. にほんごの ほんは いくらですか。

よんせん えん です

第3課 1 Verb Conjugation

▶ Memorize the thirteen verbs introduced in Lesson 3. Read the explanation about verb conjugation and complete the following tables.

Ru-verbs 〜ます 〜ません

	dictionary form	present affirmative	present negative
1. get up	おきる	おきます	おきません
2. see	みる / 見る	みます	みません
3. eat	たべる / 食べる	たべます	たべません
4. sleep	ねる / 寝る	ねます	ねません

U-verbs

	dictionary form	present affirmative	present negative
5. speak	はなす / 話す	はなします	はなしません
6. listen	きく	ききます	ききません
7. go	いく / 行く	いきます	いきません
8. read	よむ	よみます	よみません
9. drink	のむ	のみます	のみません
10. return	かえる	かえります	かえりません

Irregular Verbs

	dictionary form	present affirmative	present negative
11. come	くる	きます	きません
12. do	する	します	しません
13. study	べんきょうする	べんきょうします	べんきょうしません

第3課 2 Noun を Verb

▶ Write a ます and ません sentence using two of the nouns in each group and a verb of your choice.

Example:

> Noun:　さかな　　にく　　やさい

> affirmative　→　わたしは やさいを たべます。
> negative　　→　わたしは にくを たべません。

1. Noun:　おさけ　　おちゃ　　コーヒー

affirmative → わたしは おさけ を のみます

negative → コーヒー を のみません

2. Noun:　にほんの えいが　　アメリカの えいが　　インド (India) の えいが

affirmative → にほんのえいが を みます

negative → アメリカのえいが をみません

3. Noun:　テニス　　サッカー (soccer)　　バスケットボール (basketball)

affirmative → テニス を します

negative → サッカー を しません

4. Noun:　ほん　　おんがくの ざっし　　スポーツの ざっし

affirmative → ほん を よみます

negative → おんがくの ざっし を よみません

5. Noun:　にほんの おんがく　　ロック (rock)　　クラシック (classic)

affirmative → にほん の おんがく を ききます

negative → クラシック を ききません

第3課 3 Verbs with Places

(I) Where do the following activities take place? Add the places and appropriate particles to the following sentences.

Example: <u>としょかんで</u> ほんを よみます。

1. <u>としょかん で</u> べんきょうします。

2. <u>うち ~~は~~ で</u> テレビを みます。

3. <u>うち で</u> コーヒーを のみます。

4. <u>いえ ~~を~~ に</u> いきます。

5. <u>うち に</u> かえります。

(II) Translate the following sentences into Japanese.

1. Mr. Tanaka will go to the library.

たなか さん は としょかん に いきます

2. My friend will come to Japan.

ともたち は にほん へ ~~も~~ かえります

3. Mr. Suzuki listens to music at home.

すずき さん は うちで おんがく を ききます

4. I speak Japanese at home.

わたしは うちで にほんご が はな~~し~~ます

5. I don't eat lunch at school.

がっこうで ひるごはん を たべません

第3課 4 Time References

(I) Time Expressions—Read Grammar 4 (pp. 91-92) on time references, and classify the words below into two groups. If the words are *always* used with に, write に after the words.

1. こんばん<u>に</u>　　　　4. いつ<u>—</u>　　　　7. どようび<u>に</u>　　　10. まいにち<u>—</u>

2. しゅうまつ<u>に</u>　　5. きょう<u>—</u>　　　8. あした<u>—</u>　　　11. まいばん<u>—</u>

3. あさ<u>に</u>　　　　　6. いま<u>—</u>　　　　9. じゅういちじ<u>—</u>

(II) Your Day—Describe what you do on a typical day. Include the descriptions of activities listed below. Whenever possible, include place and time expressions. Refer to Grammar 6 (pp. 92-93) on the basic order of phrases.

おきる　　いく　　たべる　　べんきょうする　　かえる　　ねる

1. わたしは まいにち _____じに _____ます。

2.

3.

4.

5.

(III) Translate the following sentences into Japanese.

1. I speak Japanese every day.

2. I will not watch TV tonight.

3. Mary does not come to school on Saturdays.

第3課 5 Suggestion Using 〜ませんか

(I) Study the Dialogue I (p. 84) and translate the following conversation.

メアリー：1. _____
(Would you like to see a movie tonight?)

たけし ：2. _____
(Tonight is not a very good time . . .)

メアリー：3. _____
(How about tomorrow?)

たけし ：4. _____
(Sounds great.)

(II) Imagine you ask someone out. Write the dialogue between you and your friend.

You: 1. _____

Friend: 2. _____

You: 3. _____

Friend: 4. _____

第3課 6 Frequency Adverbs

▶ Translate the following sentences into Japanese.

1. I often go to the library.

   わたしは _____ としょかん _____ _____。

2. Yumi often comes to my house.

3. I usually get up at six.

4. Professor Yamashita usually goes to sleep at eleven.

5. I sometimes read Japanese newspapers.

6. Takeshi sometimes drinks coffee at that coffee shop.

7. Mary does not eat much.

第3課 7 聞く練習 (Listening Comprehension)
き　れんしゅう

(A) Listen to the dialogue between Sue and Mary. Where will they be? What will they do? Choose from the list below. 🔊 W03-A　　　*レストラン (restaurant)

		<Saturday>		<Sunday>	
		Where	What	Where	What
	Mary				
	Sue				

Where:

a. school	b. library	c. home
d. Osaka	e. Tokyo	f. Kyoto

What:

g. read a book	h. play sports	i. study
j. see a movie	k. eat dinner	

(B) Listen to the dialogue at an evening meeting at a summer camp. The group leader and the students are discussing the schedule for the next day. Complete the schedule below. 🔊 W03-B　　　*スケジュール (schedule)　ヨガ (yoga)

1. 6:00 A.M. ( )	6. 3:00 P.M. ( )
2. 7:30 ( )	7. 6:00 ( )
3. 9:00 ( )	8. 7:30 ( )
4. 12:30 P.M. ( )	9. 11:30 ( )
5. 1:30 ( )	

a. breakfast	b. dinner	c. get up	d. go to bed	e. lunch
f. do yoga	g. play tennis	h. study	i. watch a movie	

Ⓒ Listen to the dialogue between Sue and her friend. How often does she do the following things? 🔊 W03-C
(a = every day, b = often, c = sometimes, d = not often, e = not at all)

1. (　　　) study Japanese

2. (　　　) go to the library

3. (　　　) watch American movies

4. (　　　) watch Japanese movies

5. (　　　) play tennis

6. (　　　) drink coffee

Ⓓ Listen to the dialogue between Mary and a Japanese friend of hers and answer the questions below. 🔊 W03-D

1. What time is it?　　(　　　)

　　a. Eight　　b. Nine　　c. Ten　　d. Eleven

2. What did the man suggest first?　　(　　　)

　　a. Coffee at a coffee shop　　b. Beer at a bar　　c. Coffee at his place　　d. Lunch

3. How did Mary turn down his suggestion? (Mark ○ for all that apply.)

　　a. (　　　) By saying that she needs to go back home

　　b. (　　　) By saying that it is too late

　　c. (　　　) By saying that she needs to study

　　d. (　　　) By saying that she needs to go to sleep early

4. What other suggestions did the man make? (Mark ○ for all that apply.)

　　a. (　　　) Reading Japanese books together

　　b. (　　　) Practicing Japanese at a coffee shop

　　c. (　　　) Having lunch together the next day

　　d. (　　　) Walking her home

第3課 8 答えましょう (Questions)

▶Answer the following questions in Japanese.

1. よく スポーツを しますか。

2. よく えいがを みますか。

3. よく なにを のみますか。

4. おんがくは よく なにを ききますか。

5. どこで べんきょうしますか。

6. しゅうまつは よく どこに いきますか。

7. しゅうまつは よく なにを しますか。

8. なんじごろ おきますか。

9. なんじごろ ねますか。

第4課 1 Xがあります/います

(I) Translate the following sentences into Japanese.

1. There is a bus stop over there.

2. There will be no class on Thursday.

3. I do not have a dictionary. (lit., There is not a dictionary.)

4. There is Professor Yamashita over there.

5. I have a child. (lit., There is a child.)

(II) Answer the following questions in Japanese.

1. あした、アルバイトがありますか。

2. いつ日本語のクラスがありますか。
　　　に ほん ご

3. 日本に友だちがいますか。
　　に ほん　　とも

4. 兄弟 (brothers and sisters) がいますか。
　　きょうだい

```
おねえさん : older sister
いもうと : younger sister
おにいさん : older brother
おとうと : younger brother
```

第4課 2 Describing Where Things Are

(I) Draw a picture showing the items mentioned in the passage below, each in correct geometrical relation to the others.

辞書はつくえの上です。時計もつくえの上です。ぼうしは辞書と時計の間です。かばんはつくえの下です。つくえはテレビの近くです。

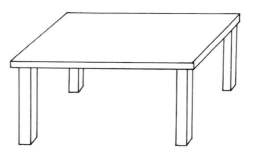

(II) Look at the pictures and answer the following questions.

1. 日本語の本はどこですか。

2. メアリーさんのかさはどこですか。

3. スーさんの辞書はどこですか。

4. 図書館はどこですか。

5. 銀行はどこですか。

1. Japanese book

2. Mary's umbrella

3. Sue's dictionary — Dictionary

4. 5.

Library

Bank

Post Office

第4課 3 Past Tense (Nouns)

(I) Answer the following questions.

1. きのうは月曜日でしたか。

2. きのうは十五日でしたか。

3. 今日の朝ご飯はハンバーガーでしたか。

4. 子供の時、いい子供でしたか。

5. 高校の時、いい学生でしたか。

(II) Translate the following sentences into Japanese.

1. My bicycle was 30,000 yen.

2. Yesterday was Sunday.

3. Professor Yamashita was not a Nihon University student.

第4課 | 4 | Verb Conjugation (Past Tense)

▶ Fill in the conjugation table below. If you are unclear about the *u*-verb/*ru*-verb distinction, read Grammar 1 in Lesson 3 (pp. 88-89) once again. If you are unclear about the past tense conjugation, refer to the table on p. 110.

U-verbs

	dictionary form	past affirmative	past negative
1. drink			
2. speak			
3. listen			
4. buy			
5. take			
6. write			
7. wait			
8. there is			

Ru-verbs and Irregular Verbs

	dictionary form	past affirmative	past negative
9. eat			
10. get up			
11. do			
12. come			

第4課 5 Past Tense (Verbs)

Ⅰ The pictures below show what Takeshi did last weekend. Answer the following questions in Japanese.

<Friday>   <Saturday>   <Sunday>

home   supermarket   town

1. たけしさんは金曜日に手紙を書きましたか。

2. たけしさんは土曜日にどこでアルバイトをしましたか。

3. たけしさんはいつ音楽を聞きましたか。

4. たけしさんは日曜日に何をしましたか。(Fill in the blanks.)

   たけしさんは_____に_____で

   _____と_____を_____。

5. あなたは、週末、何をしましたか。

Ⅱ Translate the following sentences into Japanese.

1. Yumi did not take pictures at all.

2. I often ate hamburgers when I was a child.

3. Takeshi did not study much when he was in high school.

第4課　6　も

▶ Translate the sentences into Japanese. Note that the particle も replaces は, が, and を, but goes side by side with other particles.

1. Mary went to the park. Takeshi went to the park, too.

2. There is a bookstore over there. There is a restaurant, too.

3. I drink tea. I drink coffee, too.

4. Mary will go to Korea. She will go to China, too.

5. Michiko ate hamburgers on Friday. She ate hamburgers on Saturday, too.

6. Yumi bought souvenirs at a temple. She bought souvenirs at a department store, too.

7. I took pictures at school yesterday. I took pictures at home, too.

第4課 7 ～時間・Particles
じかん

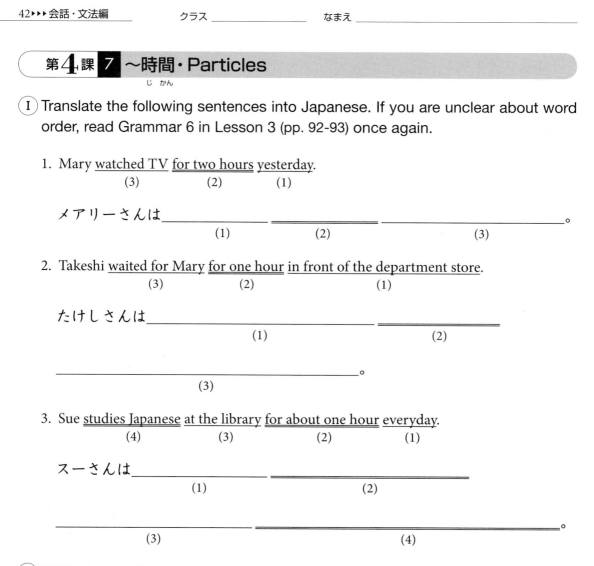

(I) Translate the following sentences into Japanese. If you are unclear about word order, read Grammar 6 in Lesson 3 (pp. 92-93) once again.

1. Mary <u>watched TV</u> <u>for two hours</u> <u>yesterday</u>.
        (3)   (2)   (1)

   メアリーさんは_____ _____ _____。
                  (1)   (2)   (3)

2. Takeshi <u>waited for Mary</u> <u>for one hour</u> <u>in front of the department store</u>.
         (3)   (2)   (1)

   たけしさんは_____ _____
                    (1)   (2)

   _____。
             (3)

3. Sue <u>studies Japanese</u> <u>at the library</u> <u>for about one hour</u> <u>everyday</u>.
        (4)   (3)   (2)   (1)

   スーさんは_____ _____
               (1)   (2)

   _____ _____。
         (3)   (4)

(II) Fill in the particles that are missing. You may want to refer to the Vocabulary section (p. 105), where the particle that goes with each of the new verbs is shown in the parentheses.

1. 私はあした友だち_____会います。
   わたし   とも   あ

2. メアリーさんは京都のお寺で写真_____撮りました。
              きょうと   てら しゃしん   と

3. 私は喫茶店でロバートさん_____待ちました。
   わたし きっさてん   ま

4. スーパーで肉_____買いました。
          にく   か

5. 私は中国語_____わかりません。
   わたし ちゅうごくご

6. 私はきのう手紙_____書きませんでした。
   わたし   てがみ   か

第4課 8 聞く練習 (Listening Comprehension)
き　　れんしゅう

(A) Mary is talking with her homestay father. Listen to the dialogue and answer the questions in Japanese. 🔊 W04-A

1. お父さんは今日何をしましたか。　_____
とう　　　　きょう なに

2. お母さんは何をしましたか。　_____
かあ　　　　なに

3. メアリーさんとお父さんはあした何をしますか。　_____
とう　　　　　なに

(B) Mary is showing a picture that she took at a party. Identify the following people.

🔊 W04-B

1. (　　　) Ken

2. (　　　) Rika

3. (　　　) Mike

4. (　　　) Takeshi

5. (　　　) Mother

6. (　　　) Father

(C) Listen to the dialogue in the classroom and answer the following questions.

＊カラオケ (karaoke) 🔊 W04-C

1. What is the date today? Choose the answer.

　a. September 8　　　b. September 10　　　c. September 14　　　d. September 18

2. What day is today? Choose the answer.

　a. Sunday　　　b. Monday　　　c. Tuesday　　　d. Wednesday

　e. Thursday　　　f. Friday　　　g. Saturday

3. Who did these things? Mark ◯ for the things they did.

	studied	took photos	went to Tokyo	wrote a letter	went to karaoke	did shopping
Sue						
Mary						
Robert						

第4課 ⑨ 答えましょう (Questions)
こた

▶Answer the following questions in Japanese.

1. あなたの家はどこですか。
　　　　　いえ

2. あなたの町に何がありますか。
　　　　　まち　なに

3. 猫／犬がいますか。名前は何ですか。
　ねこ　いぬ　　　　　　なまえ　なん

4. 今日は何月何日ですか。何曜日ですか。
　きょう　なんがつなんにち　　　なんようび

5. きのう、だれと晩ご飯を食べましたか。
　　　　　　　　　ばん　はん　た

6. きのう、何時間勉強しましたか。
　　　　　なんじかんべんきょう

7. 何曜日に日本語のクラスがありますか。
　なんようび　にほんご

8. 先週の週末、何をしましたか。
　せんしゅう　しゅうまつ　なに

第5課 1 Adjective Conjugation (Present Tense)

▶ Fill in the conjugation table below.

い-adjectives

	dictionary form	present affirmative	present negative
1. large			
2. expensive			
3. frightening			
4. interesting			
5. old			
6. good			

な-adjectives

	dictionary form	present affirmative	present negative
7. quiet			
8. beautiful			
9. healthy			
10. fond of			
11. disgusted			
12. lively			

第5課 2 Adjectives (Present Tense)

(Ⅰ) Answer the questions.

1. 日本語の宿題はやさしいですか。
   にほんご　　しゅくだい

2. 今日は忙しいですか。
   きょう　　いそが

3. あなたの部屋はきれいですか。
   へや

4. 日本語のクラスはおもしろいですか。
   にほんご

5. あなたの町は静かですか。
   まち　　しず

(Ⅱ) Translate the following sentences into Japanese.

1. This watch is expensive.

2. This coffee is not delicious.

3. Professor Yamashita is energetic.

4. The weather is not good.

5. I will not be free tomorrow.

第5課 3 Adjective Conjugation (Present and Past Tenses)

▲ Fill in the conjugation table below.

い-adjectives

	present affirmative	present negative	past affirmative	past negative
1. あたらしい				
2. いそがしい				
3. さむい				
4. むずかしい				
5. ちいさい				
6. いい				

な-adjectives

	present affirmative	present negative	past affirmative	past negative
7. ひま (な)				
8. にぎやか (な)				
9. すき (な)				
10. きれい (な)				

第5課 4 Adjectives (Past Tense)

(I) Answer the questions.

1. 先週はひまでしたか。
   せんしゅう

2. テストは難しかったですか。
   むずか

3. きのうは暑かったですか。
   あつ

4. 週末は楽しかったですか。
   しゅうまつ　　たの

5. きのうの晩ご飯はおいしかったですか。
   ばん　はん

(II) Translate the following sentences into Japanese.

1. I was busy yesterday.

2. The homework was difficult.

3. My room was not clean.

4. The weather was good.

5. The trip was not fun.

6. The tickets were not expensive.

第5課 5 Adjective + Noun

(I) Look at the pictures and answer the questions.

Ex.   1.   2.   3.   4.

small   old   quiet   scary   beautiful

Example: Q：どんな部屋ですか。   A：小さい部屋です。
　　　　　　　　　　　へや　　　　　　　　　　　　ちい　　へ や

1. Q：どんな自転車ですか。   A：
　　　　　じ てんしゃ

2. Q：どんな町ですか。   A：
　　　　　まち

3. Q：どんな人ですか。   A：
　　　　　ひと

4. Q：どんな家ですか。   A：
　　　　　いえ

(II) Translate the following sentences.

1. I met a kind person.

2. I bought an inexpensive ticket.

3. I read an interesting book last week.

第5課 6 好き（な）/きらい（な）

▶ Write down the sentences telling if you like/dislike the things below. Use 好き（な） for "like" and きらい（な） for "don't like." Use 大～ for emphasis.

Example:　homework　→　私は宿題が大好きです。

1. Japanese class

　　→

2. this town

　　→

3. Mondays

　　→

4. ocean

　　→

5. cats

　　→

6. cold mornings

　　→

7. fish

　　→

8. frightening movies

　　→

9. (your own sentence)

　　→

第5課 7 ～ましょう

(Ⅰ) You and your friend will spend one day together. Complete the underlined parts with ましょう.

友だち：どこに行きますか。
とも　　　　　　　い

私　：　1._____
わたし

友だち：いいですね。そこで何をしますか。
とも　　　　　　　　　　　　なに

私　：　2._____。それから、
わたし

　　　　3._____

友だち：何時に会いますか。
とも　　なんじ　あ

私　：　4._____
わたし

(Ⅱ) Translate the following sentences into Japanese.

1. Let's take pictures here.

2. Let's watch this movie tonight.

3. Let's wait in the coffee shop.

4. This kanji is difficult. Let's ask our teacher.

5. Let's do the homework together.

第5課 8 聞く練習 (Listening Comprehension)
き　　れんしゅう

Ⓐ Listen to the dialogue between a real estate agent and his customer and choose the appropriate answers. 🔊 W05-A　　　　＊一か月 (one month)
いっ　げつ

1. The house is [a. new / b. old].

2. The house is [a. clean / b. not clean].

3. The house is [a. quiet / b. not quiet].

4. The rooms are [a. big / b. not big].

5. There are [a. many / b. not many] rooms.

6. The rent is [a. 90,400 / b. 94,000] yen a month.

Ⓑ Listen to the TV game show "Who's My Date?" Three men want to invite Ms. Suzuki on a date. 🔊 W05-B　　　　＊おめでとうございます (Congratulations.)

1. Fill in the blanks in Japanese.

	Favorite type	What he does on holidays
吉田 よし だ		
川口 かわぐち		
中山 なかやま		

2. Who did Ms. Suzuki choose?　　[a. 吉田　　b. 川口　　c. 中山]
　　　　　　　　　　　　　　　　　　　よし だ　　　かわぐち　　　なかやま

Ⓒ Listen to the interview with Mary and Takeshi and fill in the chart with the following letters: a = likes, b = doesn't like very much, c = hates. 🔊 W05-C

	J-Pop （Jポップ）	Rock （ロック）	Classical music （クラシック）	Action movies （アクション）	Horror movies （ホラー）
😊 Mary					——
😊 Takeshi					

第5課 9 答えましょう (Questions)

(I) Answer the following questions in Japanese regarding your best trip.

1. どこに行きましたか。

2. だれと行きましたか。

3. 天気はどうでしたか。

4. 食べ物はどうでしたか。

5. そこで何をしましたか。

6. おみやげを買いましたか。

(II) Answer the following questions in Japanese.

1. どんな食べ物が好きですか。

2. どんな飲み物が好きですか。

3. どんな音楽が好きですか。

第6課 1 *Te*-form —1

▶ Review Grammar 1 (pp. 150-151) and conjugate the verbs below into their respective *te*-forms. The numbers indicate the lesson in which the verbs first appeared.

Ru-verbs

1. おきる (3)　→

2. たべる (3)　→

3. ねる (3)　　→

4. みる (3)　　→

5. いる (4)　　→

6. でかける (5) →

U-verbs ending with う

7. あう (4)　　→

8. かう (4)　　→

U-verbs ending with く

9. きく (3)　　→

10. かく (4)　　→

U-verb ending with く (irregular)

11. いく (3)　　→

U-verb ending with ぐ

12. およぐ (5) →

U-verb ending with す

13. はなす (3)　→

U-verb ending with つ

14. まつ (4)　　→

U-verbs ending with む

15. のむ (3)　　→

16. よむ (3)　　→

U-verbs ending with る

17. かえる (3)　→

18. ある (4)　　→

19. とる (4)　　→

20. わかる (4)　→

21. のる (5)　　→

22. やる (5)　　→

Irregular Verbs

23. くる (3)　　→

24. する (3)　　→

25. べんきょうする (3)→

第6課 2 Te-form —2

▶ Review the Vocabulary section (pp. 148-149) and the Grammar (pp. 150-151) and fill in the following table.

Ru-verbs

	dictionary form	*te*-form	long form（〜ます）
1. to open			
2. to teach			
3. to get off			
4. to borrow			
5. to close			
6. to take a shower			
7. to turn on			
8. to make a phone call			
9. to forget			

U-verbs

	dictionary form	*te*-form	long form（〜ます）
10. to smoke			
11. to use			
12. to help			

13. to hurry			

	dictionary form	*te*-form	long form（〜ます）
14. to return (a thing)			
15. to turn off			

16. to stand up			
17. to carry			

18. to die			

19. to play			

20. to be absent			

21. to sit down			
22. to enter			

Irregular Verbs

	dictionary form	*te*-form	long form（〜ます）
23. to bring (a person)			
24. to bring (a thing)			

第6課 3 ～てください

(I) Write what each person says using ～てください.

1. take a picture

2. teach this kanji

3. carry this bag

4. use this towel（タオル）

5. sit down

6. bring a book

1. _____

2. _____

3. _____

4. _____

5. _____

6. _____

(II) Write three request sentences using ～てください. Indicate in the parentheses who you are going to ask to do those things.

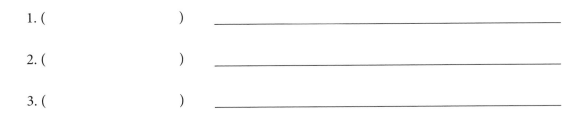

1. (　　　　　　　　) _____

2. (　　　　　　　　) _____

3. (　　　　　　　　) _____

第**6**課 4 ～てもいいです

▶ Ask the following people if it is okay to do the following things, using ～てもいいですか.

(To your friend at your friend's apartment)

1. to enter the room

2. to look at the pictures

3. to turn on the TV

4. (your own)

(To your teacher in class)

5. to go to the restroom

6. to speak English

7. to borrow a textbook

8. (your own)

第6課 5 〜てはいけません

(I) Look at the signs and make sentences using 〜てはいけません.

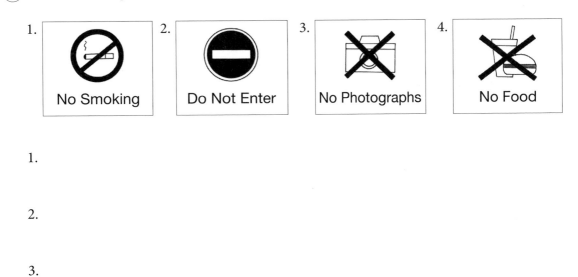

| 1. No Smoking | 2. Do Not Enter | 3. No Photographs | 4. No Food |

1.

2.

3.

4.

(II) Describe three things that you are prohibited from doing at some places.

Example:　りょう (dorm) でパーティーをしてはいけません。

1.

2.

3.

第6課 | 6 Describing Two Activities

(I) The pictures below describe what Takeshi did yesterday. Make sentences using *te*-forms.

1.

2.

3.

4.

(II) Translate the following sentences.

1. I will go to the library and return the book tomorrow.

2. Mary and Takeshi met and talked for about an hour.

3. Let's enter the coffee shop and rest.

第6課 7 ～から

(Ⅰ) Translate the following sentences, using ～から.

1. I am not free today. (It's) because I have a test tomorrow.

2. The test was not difficult. (That was) because I had studied a lot.

3. Let's go out tonight. (It's) because tomorrow is a holiday.

4. I helped my mother. (It's) because she was busy.

5. I will not drink coffee. (It's) because I drank coffee in the morning.

(Ⅱ) Complete the dialogues below.

(1) A ：あしたクラスに行きません。

　　B ：どうしてですか。

　　A ：1._____から。

(2) A ：2._____

　　B ：どうしてですか。

　　A ：3._____から。

第6課 8 聞く練習 (Listening Comprehension)
<small>き　れんしゅう</small>

(A) Listen to the dialogue at a youth hostel. Mark ○ if the following statements are true. Mark ✕ if not true. 🔊 W06-A　　　＊コインランドリー (coin laundry)

1. (　　　) The breakfast starts at 6:30.
2. (　　　) Smoking is not permitted in the room.
3. (　　　) You can take a shower in the morning.
4. (　　　) There is no coin laundry here.

(B) Your roommate has gone away for a week. She has left a message on your answering machine. Listen to it and mark ○ for what you are asked to do.

＊れいぞうこ (refrigerator)　🔊 W06-B

You are asked to:

1. (　　　) open the window
2. (　　　) water the plants
3. (　　　) drink milk
4. (　　　) return a book to Mary
5. (　　　) borrow a notebook from Robert
6. (　　　) do some shopping for a party

(C) Takeshi is trying to organize a picnic. Listen to the dialogue and answer the questions in Japanese. 🔊 W06-C　　　＊ピクニック (picnic)

1. When is NOT convenient for each of them? Why?

	a. Inconvenient day	b. Reasons
みちこ		
スー		
ロバート		

2. いつピクニックに行きますか。 ＿＿＿＿＿＿＿＿＿＿＿＿＿＿＿＿＿
<small>い</small>

第6課 9 答えましょう (Questions)
こた

▶ Answer the following questions in Japanese.

1. 朝起きて、何をしますか。
   あさお　　なに

2. きのう、家に帰って何をしましたか。
   いえ　かえ　　なに

3. テストの時、教科書を見てもいいですか。
   とき　きょうかしょ　み

4. 飛行機の中で何をしてはいけませんか。
   ひこうき　なか　なに

5. 子供の時、よく勉強しましたか。
   こども　とき　　べんきょう

6. 子供の時、よくゲームをしましたか。
   こども　とき

7. 高校の時、よく何をしましたか。
   こうこう　とき　　なに

第7課 1 *Te*-form

▶ Decide whether they are *u*-, *ru*-, or irregular verbs and fill in the table below.

	u/ru/ irregular	long form	*te*-form
Ex. ある	*u*	あります	あって
1. わかる			
2. やる			
3. けす			
4. たつ			
5. おきる			
6. かえる			
7. くる			
8. する			
9. あそぶ			
10. かける			
11. きる			
12. かぶる			
13. つとめる			
14. はく			
15. うたう			
16. すむ			
17. けっこんする			

第7課 2 ～ている (Actions in Progress)

Ⅰ Describe the following pictures, using ～ています.

1.

2.

3.

4.

5.

Ⅱ Answer the following questions in Japanese.

1. 今、何をしていますか。
   いま　なに

2. きのうの午後八時ごろ何をしていましたか。
   ご　ご　はち　じ　　なに

Ⅲ Translate the following sentences.

1. Mary is waiting for a bus at the bus stop.

2. At two o'clock yesterday, Takeshi was playing tennis with a friend.

3. I called home. My older sister was doing her homework.

第7課 3 ～ている (Result of a Change)

Ⓘ This is Michiko's family. Answer the following questions in Japanese.

Father
51, lives in Nagano,
works for a bank

Mother
47, lives in Nagano,
works for a hospital

Older sister
23, lives in Tokyo,
college student,
married

Younger brother
16, lives in Nagano,
student

1. お父さんは何をしていますか。
　　とう　　　　なに

2. お母さんは何をしていますか。
　　かあ　　　　なに

3. お姉さんは勤めていますか。
　　ねえ　　　つと

4. お姉さんは結婚していますか。
　　ねえ　　　けっこん

5. お姉さんは長野に住んでいますか。
　　ねえ　　　なが の　　す

6. 弟さんはどこに住んでいますか。
　　おとうと　　　　　　す

7. お父さんは何歳ですか。
　　とう　　　　なんさい

Ⅱ Write about your family. Try to use expressions you have learned in this lesson.

第7課 4 Describing People

(I) Translate the following sentences.

1. Yasuo is not tall.

2. Yasuo is very bright.

3. Norio is wearing a new T-shirt today.

4. Norio is skinny, but Yasuo is overweight.

やすお　のりお

(II) You are an eyewitness testifying in court. Describe the person you saw at the scene of the crime using the past tense.

1. Height:

2. Hair:

3. Glasses:

4. Eyes:

5. Clothes (above the waistline):

6. Clothes (below the waistline):

7. Shoes:

第**7**課 5 *Te*-forms for Joining Sentences

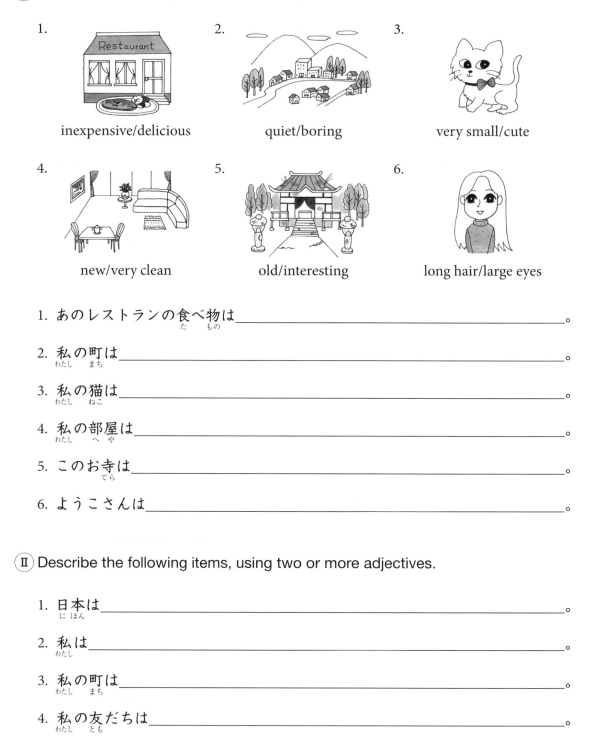

I Look at the following pictures and complete the sentences.

1.
inexpensive/delicious

2.
quiet/boring

3.
very small/cute

4.
new/very clean

5.
old/interesting

6.
long hair/large eyes

1. あのレストランの食べ物は＿＿＿＿＿＿＿＿＿＿＿＿＿＿＿＿＿＿＿＿＿＿＿＿。
　　　　　　　た　もの

2. 私の町は＿＿＿＿＿＿＿＿＿＿＿＿＿＿＿＿＿＿＿＿＿＿＿＿＿＿＿＿＿＿＿＿。
　わたし　まち

3. 私の猫は＿＿＿＿＿＿＿＿＿＿＿＿＿＿＿＿＿＿＿＿＿＿＿＿＿＿＿＿＿＿＿＿。
　わたし　ねこ

4. 私の部屋は＿＿＿＿＿＿＿＿＿＿＿＿＿＿＿＿＿＿＿＿＿＿＿＿＿＿＿＿＿＿。
　わたし　へ や

5. このお寺は＿＿＿＿＿＿＿＿＿＿＿＿＿＿＿＿＿＿＿＿＿＿＿＿＿＿＿＿＿＿＿。
　　　　てら

6. ようこさんは＿＿＿＿＿＿＿＿＿＿＿＿＿＿＿＿＿＿＿＿＿＿＿＿＿＿＿＿＿。

II Describe the following items, using two or more adjectives.

1. 日本は＿＿＿＿＿＿＿＿＿＿＿＿＿＿＿＿＿＿＿＿＿＿＿＿＿＿＿＿＿＿＿＿＿。
　に ほん

2. 私は＿＿＿＿＿＿＿＿＿＿＿＿＿＿＿＿＿＿＿＿＿＿＿＿＿＿＿＿＿＿＿＿＿＿。
　わたし

3. 私の町は＿＿＿＿＿＿＿＿＿＿＿＿＿＿＿＿＿＿＿＿＿＿＿＿＿＿＿＿＿＿＿＿。
　わたし　まち

4. 私の友だちは＿＿＿＿＿＿＿＿＿＿＿＿＿＿＿＿＿＿＿＿＿＿＿＿＿＿＿＿＿。
　わたし　とも

第7課 6 Verb Stem ＋ に 行く/来る/帰る

（ I ）Rewrite the sentences below, using the stem ＋ に行く/来る/帰る pattern.

Example:　図書館に行って、本を借ります。　→　図書館に本を借りに行きます。

1. 大阪に行って、友だちに会います。

→

2. 家に帰って、晩ご飯を食べます。

→

3. きのう、町に行って、雑誌を買いました。

→

4. 私は週末京都に行って、写真を撮りました。

→

5. ロバートさんはよく私のアパートに来て、パソコンを使います。

→

（ II ）Make your own sentences, using a place from the list below.

(Ex.) 大学	日本	食堂	喫茶店	友だちのうち	図書館	お寺	海

Example:　大学　→　大学に友だちに会いに行きます。

1.

2.

3.

4.

第7課 7 Counting People

▶ Answer the questions in Japanese.

1. 日本語のクラスに女の人が何人いますか。

2. 日本語のクラスに男の人が何人いますか。

3. 兄弟がいますか。何人いますか。

4. ルームメート (roommate) がいますか。何人いますか。

5. あなたの大学に学生が何人いますか。

6. あなたの町に人が何人住んでいますか。

7. 日本人の友だちが何人いますか。

第7課 8 聞く練習 (Listening Comprehension)
き　れんしゅう

Ⓐ One student was assaulted by someone at the dorm. A police officer is asking Robert what he and the other students were doing at the time of the incident. Write in Japanese what the following people were doing. 🔊 W07-A ＊ほかの (other)

1. ロバートさんは、 ＿＿＿＿＿＿＿＿＿＿＿＿＿＿＿＿＿＿＿＿＿＿＿＿＿＿＿

2. スーさんは、 ＿＿＿＿＿＿＿＿＿＿＿＿＿＿＿＿＿＿＿＿＿＿＿＿＿＿＿＿＿

3. たけしさんは、 ＿＿＿＿＿＿＿＿＿＿＿＿＿＿＿＿＿＿＿＿＿＿＿＿＿＿＿

4. けんさんは、 ＿＿＿＿＿＿＿＿＿＿＿＿＿＿＿＿＿＿＿＿＿＿＿＿＿＿＿＿

5. みちこさんは、 ＿＿＿＿＿＿＿＿＿＿＿＿＿＿＿＿＿＿＿＿＿＿＿＿＿＿

Ⓑ Listen to a TV reporter at a celebrity's party. Choose appropriate descriptions for each celebrity. 🔊 W07-B ＊ドレス (dress)　ボーイフレンド (boyfriend)

1. Arnold Stallone ( ) ( )
2. Noguchi Erika ( ) ( )
3. Matsumoto Yui ( ) ( )
4. Matsumoto Yui's new boyfriend ( ) ( )

a. wears jeans	b. wears a hat	c. wears glasses	d. has short hair
e. has long hair	f. is cute	g. is fat	h. is tall

Ⓒ Mary is interviewing people who are walking downtown on Sunday. What is each interviewee doing today? Choose the appropriate answers. 🔊 W07-C

1. Tanaka: [a. buying flowers　　b. buying cards　　c. buying a DVD]

2. Sato: [a. playing games　　b. singing songs　　c. playing sports]

3. Suzuki: [a. working at a department store　　b. seeing his younger sister
　　　　c. talking with his younger brother]

第7課 9 答えましょう (Questions)
こた

▶Circle one person from below and answer the questions in Japanese regarding him/her.

| father | mother | friend | girlfriend | boyfriend |
| others (| | |) | |

1. 名前は何ですか。
  なまえ　なん

2. 何歳ですか。
  なんさい

3. どこに住んでいますか。
  す

4. 何をしていますか。
  なに

5. 結婚していますか。
  けっこん

6. 背が高いですか。
  せ　たか

7. 髪が長いですか。
  かみ　なが

8. どんな人ですか。(about personality)
  ひと

第8課 1 Short Forms (Present Tense)

▶ Fill in the conjugation table below. Note that *ru*-verbs, *u*-verbs, and irregular verbs appear randomly on this sheet.

	dictionary form	short, negative	long, affirmative	*te*-form
Ex. eat	たべる	たべない	たべます	たべて
1. open				
2. buy				
3. sit down				
4. come				
5. die				
6. turn off				
7. study				
8. write				
9. there is				
10. drink				
11. understand				
12. wait				
13. play				
14. hurry				

第8課 2 Short Forms (Informal Speech)

Ⓘ Make informal question sentences using the cues and answer them in the negative.

Example:　(Do you) study Japanese today?

　　　　　→　Q：今日、日本語を勉強する？　A：ううん、勉強しない。
　　　　　　　　きょう　にほんご　べんきょう　　　　　　　　べんきょう

1. (Do you) often ride a bus?

　　→　Q：　　　　　　　　　　　　　A：

2. (Do you) speak Japanese every day?

　　→　Q：　　　　　　　　　　　　　A：

3. (Do you) have homework today?

　　→　Q：　　　　　　　　　　　　　A：

4. (Will you) go out this weekend?

　　→　Q：　　　　　　　　　　　　　A：

5. Are you free tomorrow?

　　→　Q：　　　　　　　　　　　　　A：

6. Are you Japanese?

　　→　Q：　　　　　　　　　　　　　A：

7. Is it hot?

　　→　Q：　　　　　　　　　　　　　A：

Ⓘ Answer the following questions in informal speech.

1. 今日は何曜日？
　　きょう　なんようび

2. どんな食べ物がきらい？
　　　　た　もの

3. 今週の週末、何をする？
　　こんしゅう　しゅうまつ　なに

第8課 3 Quotations（〜と思います）

(Ⅰ) Translate the following sentences. In sentences 4-6, "I don't think . . ." should be translated as 〜ないと思います.

1. I think Professor Yamashita is good-looking.

2. I think this woman is Mary's Japanese teacher.

3. I think Professor Yamashita reads many books.

4. I don't think this town is interesting. (lit., I think this town is not interesting.)

5. I don't think Mai likes Mayumi.

6. I don't think Aya will come to school today.

(Ⅱ) Answer the following questions, using 〜と思います.

1. あしたはどんな天気ですか。

2. 来週は忙しいですか。

3. あなたの日本語の先生は、料理が上手ですか。

4. あなたの日本語の先生は、今週の週末、何をしますか。

第8課 4 Quotations（〜と言っていました）

▶ Ask someone (preferably Japanese) the following questions. Report the answers using 〜と言っていました.

Example:　大学生ですか。　→　田中さんは大学生だと言っていました。

1. 毎日、楽しいですか。

→

2. どんな料理が好きですか。

→

3. お酒を飲みますか。

→

4. どんなスポーツをよくしますか。

→

5. 兄弟がいますか。

→

6. どこに住んでいますか。

→

7. 結婚していますか。

→

8. 車を持っていますか。

→

9. 週末はたいてい何をしますか。

→

10. (your own question)

→

Get the signature of the person you interviewed: ＿＿＿＿＿＿＿＿＿＿＿＿＿＿＿＿＿＿＿

第8課 5 ～ないでください

(I) Translate the following sentences.

Example:　Please don't wait for me. (Because) I will be late.

→　私を待たないでください。遅くなりますから。
　　わたし　ま　　　　　　　　　　おそ

1. Please don't forget your umbrella. (Because) It will rain this afternoon.

→

2. Please don't open the window. (Because) I am cold.

→

3. Please don't turn off the TV. (Because) I'm watching the news (ニュース).

→

4. Please don't throw away the magazine. (Because) It's not my magazine.

→

(II) Write the dictionary form of each of the verbs used in the following sentences.

Example: かけないでください。　→　___かける___

1. きらないでください。　　　_____

2. きないでください。　　　　_____

3. こないでください。　　　　_____

4. かかないでください。　　　_____

5. しないでください。　　　　_____

6. しなないでください。　　　_____

7. かえらないでください。　　_____

8. かわないでください。　　　_____

第8課 6 Verb のが好きです
す

(I) Write what you are good at/what you are not good at/what you like to do/what you don't like to do, using the verbs in the box.

speaking Japanese	driving a car	taking pictures	singing
listening to music	taking a bath	playing sports	cooking
doing laundry	cleaning	washing a car	

1. 私は＿＿＿＿＿＿＿＿＿＿＿＿＿＿＿＿＿＿下手です。
   わたし　　　　　　　　　　　　　　　　　　　　　　　　　　　　　　へ た

2. 私はあまり＿＿＿＿＿＿＿＿＿＿＿＿＿＿＿上手じゃないです。
   わたし　　　　　　　　　　　　　　　　　　　　　　　　　　　　じょう ず

3. 私は＿＿＿＿＿＿＿＿＿＿＿＿＿＿＿＿＿＿大好きです。
   わたし　　　　　　　　　　　　　　　　　　　　　　　　　　　　だい す

4. 私は＿＿＿＿＿＿＿＿＿＿＿＿＿＿＿＿＿＿きらいです。
   わたし

5. 私はあまり＿＿＿＿＿＿＿＿＿＿＿＿＿好きじゃないです。
   わたし　　　　　　　　　　　　　　　　　　　　　　　　　　　　す

(II) Translate the following sentences.

1. Erika is very good at making friends.

2. Kiyoshi loves reading books.

3. Makoto hates cleaning the room.

4. Yoshie is not good at driving a car.

5. Yuki doesn't like doing laundry very much.

第8課 7　が・何か and 何も
　　　　　　なに　　　　なに

Ⅰ Look at the picture at a party and complete the following conversations.

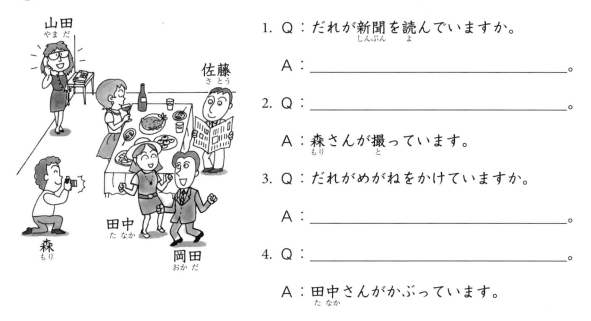

1. Q：だれが新聞を読んでいますか。
　　　　　　しんぶん　よ

　 A：＿＿＿＿＿＿＿＿＿＿＿＿＿＿＿＿＿＿＿。

2. Q：＿＿＿＿＿＿＿＿＿＿＿＿＿＿＿＿＿＿＿。

　 A：森さんが撮っています。
　　　　もり　　　　と

3. Q：だれがめがねをかけていますか。

　 A：＿＿＿＿＿＿＿＿＿＿＿＿＿＿＿＿＿＿＿。

4. Q：＿＿＿＿＿＿＿＿＿＿＿＿＿＿＿＿＿＿＿。

　 A：田中さんがかぶっています。
　　　　たなか

Ⅱ Translate the following sentences.
(Note especially that 何か and 何も are normally not accompanied by particles.)
　　　　　　　　　　　なに　　　　　なに

　1. Q：Did you eat anything this morning?

　　 A：No, I did not eat anything this morning.

　2. Q：What will you do over the weekend?

　　 A：I won't do anything.

　3. Yoshio asked something, but I did not understand.

　4. Would you like to drink anything?

第8課 8 聞く練習 (Listening Comprehension)
き　　れんしゅう

(A) Choose the picture that describes the situation in which you are likely to hear each of the sentences. [剝)) W08-A

1. (　　)　　2. (　　)　　3. (　　)　　4. (　　)　　5. (　　)　　6. (　　)　　7. (　　)

(B) Robert and Ken are talking. Answer the questions in Japanese. [剝)) W08-B

1. ロバートさんとけんさんは、いつゲームをしますか。

2. たけしさんはゲームをしに来ますか。どうしてですか。
　　　　　　　　　　　　　　き

3. トムさんはゲームをしに来ますか。どうしてですか。
　　　　　　　　　き

(C) Mary is reporting her interview with Professor Honma to the class. Circle every item that is true according to Mary's interview. [剝)) W08-C　　＊インタビュー (interview)

1. Prof. Honma likes a woman who is:

[a. pretty　　b. tall　　c. short　　d. gentle　　e. smart　　f. slim].

2. He spends his weekends:

[a. playing baseball　　b. playing tennis　　c. watching sports games　　d. dating].

3. His students in a Japanese class are:

[a. lively　　b. quiet　　c. diligent　　d. kind　　e. interesting].

第8課 9 答えましょう (Questions)

Ⅰ Answer the following questions in Japanese using 〜と思います.

1. 日本語のクラスについてどう思いますか。

2. 日本語の先生は何をするのが好きですか。

3. あした、雨が降りますか。

4. あなたの友だちは料理が上手ですか。

Ⅱ Answer the following questions in Japanese.

1. 何をするのが好きですか。

2. 何をするのが下手ですか。

3. 何をするのがきらいですか。

4. 掃除するのが好きですか。

第9課 1 Past Tense Short Forms

▶ Complete the chart below.

Verbs

dictionary form	past, affirmative	past, negative	long, present
Ex. たべる	たべた	たべなかった	たべます
1. よむ			
2. あそぶ			
3. おぼえる			
4. いく			
5. もらう			
6. おどる			
7. およぐ			
8. ひく			
9. やすむ			
10. する			
11. くる			

Adjectives/Noun

dictionary form	past, affirmative	past, negative
Ex. おもしろい	おもしろかった	おもしろくなかった
12. わかい		
13. かっこいい		
Ex. いじわる(な)	いじわるだった	いじわるじゃなかった
14. きれい(な)		
15. にちようび		

第9課 2 Past Tense Short Forms (Informal Speech)

Ⓘ Make informal question sentences using the cues and answer them in the negative.

Example: きのう、日本語を勉強する　→　Q：きのう、日本語を勉強した？

A：ううん、勉強しなかった。

1. きのう、友だちに会う

　　→　Q：　　　　　　　　　　　　　　A：

2. きのう、運動する

　　→　Q：　　　　　　　　　　　　　　A：

3. 先週、試験がある

　　→　Q：　　　　　　　　　　　　　　A：

4. 先週の週末、大学に来る

　　→　Q：　　　　　　　　　　　　　　A：

5. 先週の週末、楽しい

　　→　Q：　　　　　　　　　　　　　　A：

6. 子供の時、髪が長い

　　→　Q：　　　　　　　　　　　　　　A：

7. 子供の時、勉強がきらい

　　→　Q：　　　　　　　　　　　　　　A：

Ⅱ Make your own questions you want to ask your friend about his/her childhood in informal speech.

Example: 子供の時、よくスポーツをした？

1.

2.

3.

第**9**課 **3** Past Tense Short Forms (〜と思います)
<small>おも</small>

(Ⅰ) Translate the following sentences, using the short form + と思います. In sentences 4-6, "I don't think . . ." should be translated as 〜なかったと思います.
<small>おも</small>

1. I think Tadashi's father was good-looking when he was young.

2. I think the concert began at nine o'clock.

3. I think Saeko did physical exercises last weekend.

4. I don't think the last week's exam was difficult. (lit., I think the last week's exam was not difficult.)

5. I don't think Mie was mean when she was a child.

6. I don't think Mai received a letter from Mari.

(Ⅱ) Guess what your friends/family/teachers were like when they were children using 〜と思います.
<small>おも</small>

Example:　メアリーさんは子供の時、かわいかったと思います。
<small>こども　とき　　　　　　　　おも</small>

1.

2.

3.

第9課 4 Quotations（〜と言っていました）

▶ Ask someone (preferably Japanese) the following questions. Report the answers using 〜と言っていました.

Example: 仕事は何ですか。 → 田中さんは会社員だと言っていました。

1. どんな音楽をよく聞きますか。

→

2. 何をするのがきらいですか。

→

3. 先週の週末、何をしましたか。

→

4. 子供の時、いい子でしたか。

→

5. 子供の時、背が高かったですか。

→

6. 子供の時、学校が好きでしたか。

→

7. 子供の時、どこに住んでいましたか。

→

8. 子供の時、よく何をしましたか。

→

9. (your own question)

→

Get the signature of the person you interviewed: _____

第9課 5 Qualifying Nouns with Verbs

▶ Look at the picture and answer the questions. Use the pattern ○○さんは〜ている人です, describing what each person is currently doing.

1. みどりさんはどの人ですか。

2. けんいちさんはどの人ですか。

3. ともこさんはどの人ですか。

4. しんじさんはどの人ですか。

5. えりかさんはどの人ですか。

第9課 6 まだ〜ていません

▶ Write questions to ask if one has already done the things below. Answer the questions using もう or まだ. Note that answers to もう questions require different verb forms in the affirmative and in the negative. If you are unclear, review Grammar 3 (pp. 214-215).

Example:　eat lunch

　→　Q：もう昼ご飯を食べましたか。
　　　A：はい、もう食べました。／いいえ、まだ食べていません。

1. memorize new kanji

　→　Q：_____

　　　A：はい、_____

2. clean your room

　→　Q：_____

　　　A：いいえ、_____

3. talk with the new teacher

　→　Q：_____

　　　A：いいえ、_____

4. do homework

　→　Q：_____

　　　A：はい、_____

第9課 7 〜から

(I) Translate the following sentences. Note that [the reason＋から] precedes the result.

1. I won't do physical exercises because I am sick today.

2. I will not take a walk today because it is raining.

3. Masako is very popular because she is good at dancing.

4. I was very lonely because I did not have any friends.

(II) Answer the questions, using [the short form＋から].

Example:　　Q：きのう勉強しましたか。
　　　　　　 A：いいえ、宿題がなかったから、勉強しませんでした。

1. Q：先週は忙しかったですか。

　　A：＿＿＿＿＿＿＿＿＿＿＿＿＿＿＿＿＿＿＿＿＿＿＿＿＿＿＿＿＿＿＿＿＿。

2. Q：きのう、学校に来ましたか。

　　A：＿＿＿＿＿＿＿＿＿＿＿＿＿＿＿＿＿＿＿＿＿＿＿＿＿＿＿＿＿＿＿＿＿。

3. Q：今週の週末、出かけますか。

　　A：＿＿＿＿＿＿＿＿＿＿＿＿＿＿＿＿＿＿＿＿＿＿＿＿＿＿＿＿＿＿＿＿＿。

4. Q：来年も日本語を勉強しますか。

　　A：＿＿＿＿＿＿＿＿＿＿＿＿＿＿＿＿＿＿＿＿＿＿＿＿＿＿＿＿＿＿＿＿＿。

第9課 8 聞く練習 (Listening Comprehension)
き　れんしゅう

A Ken and Michiko are talking. Listen to the dialogue and answer the questions in Japanese. W09-A ＊イタリア (Italy)

1. だれが遅くなりましたか。
おそ

2. けんさん／みちこさんは何分ぐらい待ちましたか。
なんぷん　　　　　　　　　ま

3. けんさんとみちこさんは何をしますか。
なに

4. レストランはどこにありますか。

B Jun is showing the picture taken at his birthday party. Where are the following people in the picture? W09-B ＊ケーキ (cake)　ワイン (wine)

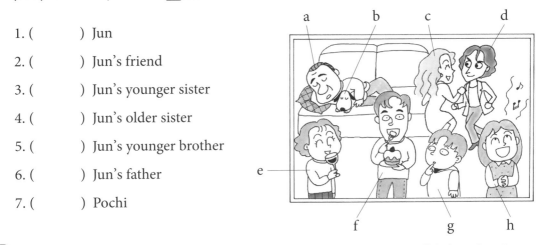

1. (　　　　) Jun
2. (　　　　) Jun's friend
3. (　　　　) Jun's younger sister
4. (　　　　) Jun's older sister
5. (　　　　) Jun's younger brother
6. (　　　　) Jun's father
7. (　　　　) Pochi

C Listen to the dialogue at a shop. How many of each item did the shopkeeper sell? W09-C

	How many?	Total amount			How many?	Total amount
1. coffee	(　　　)	¥ _____	4. tea	(　　　)	¥ _____
2. orange (オレンジ)	(　　　)	¥ _____	5. boxed lunch	(　　　)	¥ _____
3. rice ball (おにぎり)	(　　　)	¥ _____			

第9課 9 答えましょう (Questions)
こた

▶ Answer the following questions in casual style.

1. きのうの晩ご飯は何を食べた？
ばん　はん　なに　　た

　　おいしかった？

2. きのう何時ごろ寝た？
なん じ　　　ね

3. きのう洗濯した？
せんたく

4. もう十課 (Lesson 10) の単語を覚えた？
じゅっ か　　　　　　　たん ご　　おぼ

5. 先週、映画を見た？
せんしゅう　えい が　み

　　どうだった？

6. 子供の時、何をするのが好きだった？
こ ども　とき　なに　　　　　　す

7. 週末、何をした？
しゅうまつ　なに

第10課 1 Comparison between Two Items

(Ⅰ) Translate the following sentences.

1. Russia (ロシア) is larger than Canada (カナダ).

2. Sundays are more fun than Mondays.

3. Spock (スポック) is smarter than Kirk (カーク).

4. Q：Soccer and baseball, which do you like better?

   A：I like baseball better.

(Ⅱ) Make comparative sentences (both questions and answers).

Example:　Q：日本語のクラスとビジネスのクラスとどっちのほうが大変ですか。
　　　　　A：日本語のクラスのほうがビジネスのクラスより大変です。

1. Q：

   A：

2. Q：

   A：

第10課 2 Comparison among Three or More Items

(Ⅰ) Using the following categories, make "what/where/who is the most . . ." questions and answer them.

(Ex.) 日本料理 に ほんりょう り	世界の町 せ かい　まち	有名人 ゆうめいじん	季節 き せつ	野菜 や さい	外国語 がいこく ご

Example:

Q：日本料理の中で、何がいちばんおいしいですか。
　　に ほんりょうり　なか　なに

A：すしがいちばんおいしいです。／すしがいちばんおいしいと思います。
　　　　　　　　　　　　　　　　　　　　　　　　　　　　　　おも

1. Q：

　 A：

2. Q：

　 A：

3. Q：

　 A：

(Ⅱ) Make comparison sentences with the items below.

Example:　kanji / *katakana* / *hiragana*

　　　　→　漢字とカタカナとひらがなの中で、漢字がいちばん難しいです。
　　　　　　かん じ　　　　　　　　　　　　　　なか　　かん じ　　　　　　　むずか

1. Takeshi / Robert / Professor Yamashita

2. meat / fish / vegetables

第10課 3 Adjective/Noun ＋ の

Ⅰ Look at the pictures and complete the dialogue, using の.

Mary's   Takeshi's   Mary's   Takeshi's

1. Q：メアリーさんのシャツはどちらですか。

   A：＿＿＿＿＿＿＿＿＿＿＿＿＿＿＿＿＿＿＿＿＿＿＿＿＿＿＿＿＿。

2. Q：この黒いシャツは＿＿＿＿＿＿＿＿＿＿＿＿＿＿＿＿＿＿＿＿＿＿＿。

   A：たけしさんのです。

3. Q：メアリーさんのパンツはどちらですか。

   A：＿＿＿＿＿＿＿＿＿＿＿＿＿＿＿＿＿＿＿＿＿＿＿＿＿＿＿＿＿。

4. Q：この長いパンツはスーさんのですか。

   A：＿＿＿＿＿＿＿＿＿＿＿＿＿＿＿＿＿＿＿＿＿＿＿＿＿＿＿＿＿。

Ⅱ Translate the following sentences.

1. This clock is expensive. Give me a cheap one.

2. My computer is slower than yours.

3. What kind of movie do you like? —— I like scary ones.

4. This dictionary is old. I will buy a new one.

5. This red shirt is more expensive than that white one.

第10課 4 ～つもりだ

Ⅰ Make sentences using ～つもりです.

    Example: see a movie tonight

        →　今晩映画を見るつもりです。
　　　　　　　こんばんえい が　　 み

1. not go out on Sunday

    →

2. work for a Japanese company

    →

3. not get married

    →

4. study this week because we have an exam next week

    →

Ⅱ Answer the following questions, using ～つもりです.

1. 今晩何をしますか。
　 こんばんなに

2. この週末、何をしますか。
　 しゅうまつ　 なに

3. 来学期も日本語を勉強しますか。
　 らいがっ き　　に ほん ご　　べんきょう

4. 夏休み／冬休みに何をしますか。
　 なつやす　　 ふゆやす　　なに

第10課 5 Adjective ＋ なる

Ⅰ Describe the following changes, using 〜なりました.

1.   tall   2.   3.

1.

2.

3.

Ⅱ Translate the following sentences, using the verb なります. Pay attention to the order of elements in the sentences "(reason clause) から, (main clause)."

1. My room became clean, because I cleaned it this morning.

2. I have become sleepy, because I did not sleep much last night.

3. I have become very good at speaking Japanese, because I practiced a lot.

4. I will be (become) a teacher, because I like children.

第10課 6 ～で行きます/かかります・どこかに/どこにも

Ⅰ Based on the picture below, complete the following conversation.

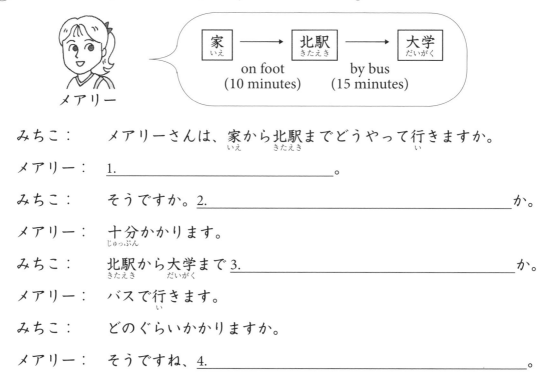

家
いえ ——→ 北駅
きたえき ——→ 大学
だいがく

on foot
(10 minutes)　　by bus
(15 minutes)

メアリー

みちこ：　　メアリーさんは、家から北駅までどうやって行きますか。
　　　　　　　　　　　　いえ　　きたえき　　　　　　　　　　　い

メアリー：　1._____。

みちこ：　　そうですか。2._____か。

メアリー：　十分かかります。
　　　　　　じゅっぷん

みちこ：　　北駅から大学まで 3._____か。
　　　　　　きたえき　　だいがく

メアリー：　バスで行きます。
　　　　　　　　　　い

みちこ：　　どのぐらいかかりますか。

メアリー：　そうですね、4._____。

Ⅱ Translate the following sentences into Japanese.

1. Q：Are you going anywhere next holiday?

   A：No, I am not going anywhere.

2. Q：Did you do anything last weekend?

   A：No, I did not do anything.

3. Q：Did you meet anyone at the party?

   A：No, I did not meet anyone.

第10課 7 聞く練習 (Listening Comprehension)

Ⓐ Mary and her friends are talking about the upcoming winter vacation. Listen to the dialogue and fill in the chart in Japanese. 🔊 W10-A

	どこに 行きますか	何をしますか	どのぐらい 行きますか
メアリー			
ロバート			
たけし			
スー			

Ⓑ Naomi, who is a student at a Japanese language school, wants to go to college in Japan. She is interested in three universities (Hanaoka, Sakura, and Tsushima). Listen to the conversation between Naomi and her Japanese teacher and answer the questions in Japanese. 🔊 W10-B ＊学費 (tuition)

1. はなおか大学とさくら大学とつしま大学の中で、どれがいちばん大きいですか。

2. つしま大学の学費はいくらですか。

3. ここからさくら大学までどのぐらいかかりますか。どうやって行きますか。

4. どの大学の日本語のクラスがいちばんいいですか。

Ⓒ Read Michiko's diary. Listen to the questions and write your answers in Japanese.

🔊 W10-C

冬休みに友だちと東京へ行った。12月11日にバスで行った。
東京で買い物をした。それから、東京ディズニーランドに
行った。12月15日に帰った。とても楽しかった。

1.

2.

3.

4.

5.

第10課 8 答えましょう (Questions)
こた

▶ Answer the following questions in Japanese.

1. 食べ物の中で何がいちばん好きですか。
   た もの なか なに す

2. 季節の中でいつがいちばん好きですか。どうしてですか。
   き せつ なか す

3. 有名人の中でだれがいちばん好きですか。どうしてですか。
   ゆうめいじん なか す

4. あなたと日本語の先生とどっちのほうが背が高いですか。
   に ほん ご せんせい せ たか

5. あなたはどうやって家から学校まで行きますか。どのぐらいかかりますか。
   いえ がっこう い

6. 今度の休みにどこかに行きますか。
   こん ど やす い

7. 先週の週末、何かしましたか。
   せんしゅう しゅうまつ なに

8. 先週の週末、だれかに会いましたか。
   せんしゅう しゅうまつ あ

第11課 1 〜たい

(Ⅰ) Choose from the list below two things you want to do and two things you don't want to do and make sentences.

山に登る　　学校をやめる　　ピアノを習う　　テレビを見る　　働く	
うそをつく　　友だちとけんかする　　外国に住む　　旅行する	

1. What you want to do:

   a.

   b.

2. What you don't want to do:

   a.

   b.

(Ⅱ) Write if you wanted or did not want to do the following things.

Example:　go to school

→　子供の時、学校に行きたかったです。／
　　子供の時、学校に行きたくなかったです。

1. own a dog

   →

2. eat snacks

   →

3. ride a train

   →

4. be a singer

   →

5. play games

   →

第11課　2　〜たり〜たりする

Ⅰ　Translate the following sentences, using 〜たり〜たり.

1. I watched a movie, shopped, etc., on the weekend.

2. I'll do laundry, study, etc., tomorrow.

3. I met a friend, read a book, etc., yesterday.

4. I practice Japanese, watch a Japanese movie, etc., at home.

5. I want to climb a mountain, go to a hot spring, etc., this weekend.

6. You must not smoke, drink beer, etc., at the dormitory (りょう).

Ⅱ　Answer the questions, using 〜たり〜たり.

1. デートの時、何をしますか。
　　　とき　なに

2. 休みに何をしましたか。
　　やす　なに

3. 子供の時、よく何をしましたか。
　　こども　とき　　なに

4. 今度の週末、何がしたいですか。
　　こんど　しゅうまつ　なに

第11課 3 〜ことがある

Ⅰ Choose from the list below three things you have done and three things you have never done and make sentences.

> 山に登る　　日本料理を作る　　英語を教える　　猫を飼う　　地下鉄に乗る
> やま のぼ　　に ほんりょう り　つく　　えい ご　 おし　　ねこ　 か　　ち か てつ　 の
> クラスで寝る　　働く　　外国に住む　　ダイエットをする　　ピアノを習う
> 　　　　　 ね　　はたら　　がいこく　 す　　　　　　　　　　　　　　　　なら
> 先生に手紙を書く　　友だちとけんかする
> せんせい　 て がみ　か　　とも

1. What you have done:

a.

b.

c.

2. What you have never done:

a.

b.

c.

Ⅱ Make questions and answers using the cues.

Example:　to tell a lie

→　Q：うそをついたことがありますか。

A：はい、あります。／いいえ、ありません。

1. to cut classes

→　Q：

A：

2. to climb Mt. Fuji（富士山）
　　　　　　　　　　　 ふ じ さん

→　Q：

A：

第11課 4 Noun A や Noun B

▶ Answer the questions with 〜や〜.

1. 大学の近くに何がありますか。
   だいがく　ちか　　　なに

2. 今、十万円あります。何が買いたいですか。
   いま　じゅうまんえん　　　　なに　か

3. 誕生日に何をもらいましたか。
   たんじょうび　なに

4. 休みの日に、よくどこに行きますか。
   やす　ひ　　　　　　　　　い

5. 有名人の中で、だれに会いたいですか。
   ゆうめいじん　なか　　　　　あ

6. どんな日本料理を食べたことがありますか。
   にほんりょうり　た

7. カラオケでどんな歌を歌いますか。
   うた　うた

第11課 5 聞く練習 (Listening Comprehension)
き　れんしゅう

Ⓐ Akira, Yoshiko, and Ken are talking about their vacation. What did they do? What are they planning to do for the next vacation? Choose the answers from the list. 🔊 W11-A   ＊ビーチ (beach)

a. skiing　　b. camping　　c. driving　　d. watching TV	
e. shopping　　f. meeting friends　　g. taking a walk on a beach	
h. working part-time　　i. climbing mountains　　j. taking a spa bath	

	1. last vacation	2. next vacation
あきら……	(　　)(　　)	(　　)
よしこ……	(　　)(　　)(　　)	(　　)
けん………	(　　)	(　　)(　　)

Ⓑ Listen to the three short dialogues and choose the most appropriate answer(s).

🔊 W11-B

1. They are going to have [a. pizza　b. sushi　c. spaghetti (スパゲッティ)].

2. They are going to watch [a. Godzilla　b. Titanic　c. E.T.　d. undecided].

3. What are they going to do in New York?

　　　Today:　　[a. shopping　b. art museum　c. movie　d. musical (ミュージカル)]

　　　Tomorrow: [a. shopping　b. art museum　c. movie　d. musical]

Ⓒ Listen to the dialogue and fill in the blanks. 🔊 W11-C

1. メアリーさんは、今、_____と言っていました。
　　　　　　　　　いま　　　　　　　　　　　　　　　　　　　　　　　い

2. トムさんは、子供の時、_____と言っていました。
　　　　　　こども　とき　　　　　　　　　　　　　　　　　　い

3. 先生は、子供の時、_____と言っていました。
　せんせい　こども　とき　　　　　　　　　　　　　　　　　い

第11課 6 答えましょう (Questions)
こた

(I) Answer the following questions about your trip in Japanese.

1. どこに行きましたか。
　　い

2. そこで何をしましたか。(Use 〜たり〜たり.)
　　　　　なに

3. 食べ物はどうでしたか。何を食べましたか。(Use や.)
　　た　もの　　　　　　　　　なに　た

4. どんな所でしたか。(Use 〜て／〜で.)
　　　　　ところ

5. また行きたいですか。どうしてですか。
　　　　い

(II) Answer the following questions in Japanese.

1. 子供の時、何になりたかったですか。
　　こども　とき　なに

2. 猫や犬を飼ったことがありますか。
　　ねこ　いぬ　か

3. 今は何になりたいですか。どうしてですか。
　　いま　なに

第12課 1 ～んです

Ⅰ Answer the question using ～んです according to the given cues.

Q：どうしたんですか。

1. A：＿＿＿＿＿＿＿＿＿＿＿＿＿＿＿＿＿＿＿。
(have a stomachache)

2. A：＿＿＿＿＿＿＿＿＿＿＿＿＿＿＿＿＿＿＿。
(broke up with my girlfriend)

3. A：＿＿＿＿＿＿＿＿＿＿＿＿＿＿＿＿＿＿＿。
(caught a cold)

4. A：＿＿＿＿＿＿＿＿＿＿＿＿＿＿＿＿＿＿＿。
(hangover)

5. A：＿＿＿＿＿＿＿＿＿＿＿＿＿＿＿＿＿＿＿。
(lost my wallet)

6. A：＿＿＿＿＿＿＿＿＿＿＿＿＿＿＿＿＿＿＿。
(the grade was bad)

Ⅱ Make up the reasons and answer the questions with ～んです.

1. Q：どうしてアルバイトをしているんですか。

A：＿＿＿＿＿＿＿＿＿＿＿＿＿＿＿＿＿＿＿。

2. Q：どうしてきのう授業をサボったんですか。

A：＿＿＿＿＿＿＿＿＿＿＿＿＿＿＿＿＿＿＿。

3. Q：どうして疲れているんですか。

A：＿＿＿＿＿＿＿＿＿＿＿＿＿＿＿＿＿＿＿。

4. Q：どうして緊張しているんですか。

A：＿＿＿＿＿＿＿＿＿＿＿＿＿＿＿＿＿＿＿。

第12課 2 ～すぎる

Ⓘ Complete the sentences according to the given cues.

1. このお菓子は_____。
   <u>か し</u>   (too sweet)

2. あの授業は_____。
   <u>じゅぎょう</u>   (too difficult)

3. 今日は_____から、学校に行きたくないです。
   <u>きょう</u>   (too cold)   <u>がっこう</u> <u>い</u>

4. 先週、_____。
   <u>せんしゅう</u>   (I worked too much)

5. きのう、_____。
                (I watched TV too much)

6. _____から、頭が痛くなりました。
          (was too nervous)   <u>あたま</u> <u>いた</u>

7. _____から、のどが痛くなりました。
       (sang songs too much)   <u>いた</u>

8. 週末_____から、今日は勉強します。
   <u>しゅうまつ</u>   (played around too much)   <u>きょう</u> <u>べんきょう</u>

Ⓘ Complain about something or somebody, using ～すぎる.

Sample topics: life / Japanese class / food in the cafeteria / your room / friend / father /
                 mother / teacher

1.

2.

　　　クラス ＿＿＿＿＿＿＿＿　　　なまえ ＿＿＿＿＿＿＿＿＿＿＿＿＿＿＿＿＿

第12課 3 〜ほうがいいです

Ⅰ Translate the following sentences.

1. You had better go to a hospital.

2. You had better memorize kanji.

3. You had better write a letter to your mother.

4. You had better not worry.

5. You had better not smoke.

6. You had better not tell a lie.

Ⅱ Give advice using 〜ほうがいいですよ.

1. Your friend：あしたテストがあるんです。

   You：＿＿＿＿＿＿＿＿＿＿＿＿＿＿＿＿＿＿＿＿＿＿＿＿＿＿＿。

2. Your friend：おなかがすいたんです。

   You：＿＿＿＿＿＿＿＿＿＿＿＿＿＿＿＿＿＿＿＿＿＿＿＿＿＿＿。

3. Your friend：かぜをひいたんです。

   You：＿＿＿＿＿＿＿＿＿＿＿＿＿＿＿＿＿＿＿＿＿＿＿＿＿＿＿。

第12課 4 〜ので

(I) Translate the following sentences, using 〜ので. Note that [the reason + ので] precedes the result.

1. I am tired, because I am busy every day.

2. I came to Japan, because I wanted to study Japanese.

3. I like her, because she is kind.

4. I read the newspaper every day, because I am interested in politics.

5. My grade was bad, because I didn't study.

6. I will not go to the party tomorrow, because I have a scheduling conflict.

(II) Answer the questions, using 〜ので.

Example:　Q：きのう勉強しましたか。
　　　　　　A：いいえ、宿題がなかったので、勉強しませんでした。

1. Q：歌手の中でだれが好きですか。

　　A：＿＿＿＿＿＿＿＿＿＿＿＿＿＿＿＿＿＿＿＿＿＿＿＿＿＿＿＿

2. Q：今どこにいちばん行きたいですか。

　　A：＿＿＿＿＿＿＿＿＿＿＿＿＿＿＿＿＿＿＿＿＿＿＿＿＿＿＿＿

3. Q：将来どんな仕事がしたいですか。

　　A：＿＿＿＿＿＿＿＿＿＿＿＿＿＿＿＿＿＿＿＿＿＿＿＿＿＿＿＿

第12課 5 ～なければいけません/なきゃいけません

(I) Read the first half of the sentences. Then, choose what you have to do from the list and complete the sentences using ～なければいけません/なきゃいけません. You may use the same words *only once*.

quit the part-time job　　buy the textbook　　do laundry　　practice　　get up early

1. あしたは九時から授業があるので、_____。
　　　　　く　じ　　　　じゅぎょう

2. 新しい授業が始まるので、_____。
　　あたら　　じゅぎょう　　はじ

3. 来週テニスの試合があるので、_____。
　　らいしゅう　　　　　し あい

4. お母さんが病気なので、_____。
　　かあ　　　　びょうき

5. 勉強が忙しくなったので、_____。
　　べんきょう　いそが

(II) Write two things you have to do this week and two things you had to do yesterday.

1. This week:

a.

b.

2. Yesterday:

a.

b.

第12課 6 ～でしょう

(Ⅰ) You are a meteorologist. Look at the table and report the weather and the temperature of each location with ～でしょう.

Tomorrow's Weather

	天気 てんき	気温 きおん
Ex. 北海道 ほっかいどう	☃	5°C
1. 東京 とうきょう	☁	17°C
2. 大阪 おおさか	☂	20°C
3. 沖縄 おきなわ	☀	24°C

Example: 北海道はあした雪でしょう。気温は五度ぐらいでしょう。
　　　　　ほっかいどう　　　ゆき　　　　　きおん　ごど

1.

2.

3.

(Ⅱ) Report tomorrow's weather of the place you live.

第12課 7 聞く練習 (Listening Comprehension)
き　れんしゅう

(A) Listen to the three dialogues at the health clinic. Mark ○ for the symptoms each patient has and write down the doctor's suggestion in Japanese. 🔊 W12-A

＊さしみ (raw fish)　ねつをはかる (take one's temperature)

Patient	sore throat	head-ache	stomach-ache	cough	fever	doctor's suggestion
1						
2						
3						

(B) Two colleagues are talking at the office. Listen to the dialogue and answer the following questions in Japanese. 🔊 W12-B

1. 男の人は今晩飲みに行きますか。どうしてですか。
おとこ　ひと　こんばん の　　い

2. 男の人はもうプレゼントを買いましたか。
おとこ　ひと　　　　　　　　　　か

(C) Listen to tomorrow's weather forecast and fill in the chart in Japanese. 🔊 W12-C

	天気 てんき	気温 きおん
1. 東京 とうきょう		℃
2. モスクワ (Moscow)		℃
3. バンコク (Bangkok)		℃
4. キャンベラ (Canberra)		℃

第12課 8 答えましょう (Questions)
こた

▶ Answer the following questions in Japanese.

1. あしたはどんな天気ですか。
　　　　　　　　てん き

2. 今、気温は何度ぐらいですか。
　　いま　き おん　なん ど

3. 今、何に興味がありますか。
　　いま　なに　きょう み

4. 日本語のクラスは宿題が多いと思いますか。
　　に ほん ご　　　　　　しゅくだい　おお　　　おも

5. 悪い成績を取ったことがありますか。
　　わる　せいせき　と

6. かぜの時、何をしたほうがいいですか。
　　　　　とき　なに

7. 今週の週末、何をしなければいけませんか。
　　こんしゅう　しゅうまつ　なに

8. どうして日本語を勉強していますか。
　　　　　に ほん ご　べんきょう

読み書き編
よ か へん

Reading and Writing Section

第1課 1 Hiragana (あ – こ)
だい いっ か

Ⅰ Practice writing the following ten *hiragana* (あ through こ).

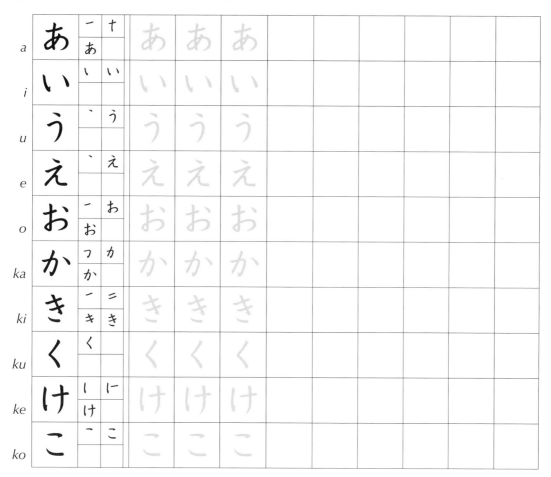

Ⅱ Copy and romanize the words below.

1. こい
(carp)

2. うえ
(above)

3. おか
(hill)

4. あき
(autumn)

5. いけ
(pond)

6. かく
(write)

Ⅲ Write the words below in *hiragana*.

1. *au*
(meet)

2. *ie*
(house)

3. *ai*
(love)

4. *kao*
(face)

5. *koe*
(voice)

6. *kiku*
(listen)

第1課 2 Hiragana (さ – と)
だい いっ か

I Practice writing the following ten *hiragana* (さ through と).

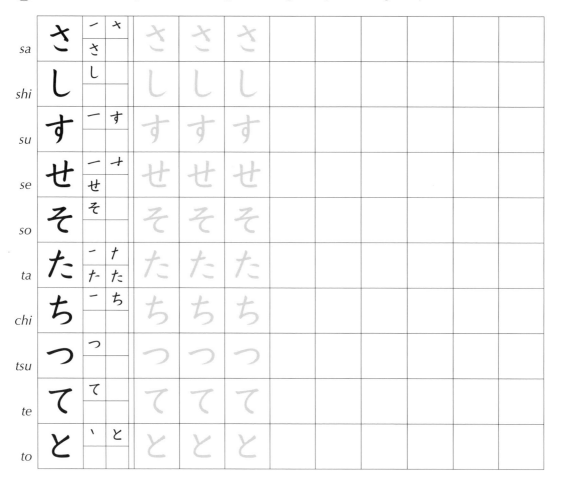

II Copy and romanize the words below.

1. あさ
(morning)

2. とち
(land)

3. かたて
(one hand)

4. すし
(name of Japanese cuisine)

5. きせつ
(season)

6. そと
(outside)

III Write the words below in *hiragana*.

1. *tasuke*
(help)

2. *chikatetsu*
(subway)

3. *sekai*
(world)

4. *kasa*
(umbrella)

5. *toshi*
(age)

6. *asoko*
(over there)

第1課 3 Hiragana (な – ほ)
だい いっ か

Ⅰ) Practice writing the following ten *hiragana* (な through ほ).

na	な	ー ナ / ナ な	な	な	な					
ni	に	し に / に	に	に	に					
nu	ぬ	し ぬ / ぬ	ぬ	ぬ	ぬ					
ne	ね	し ね / ね	ね	ね	ね					
no	の	の	の	の	の					
ha	は	し に / は	は	は	は					
hi	ひ	ひ	ひ	ひ	ひ					
fu	ふ	ゝ ぶ / ぶ ふ	ふ	ふ	ふ					
he	へ	へ	へ	へ	へ					
ho	ほ	し に / に ほ	ほ	ほ	ほ					

Ⅱ) Copy and romanize the words below.

1. ひふ
(skin)

2. なにか
(something)

3. ほね
(bone)

4. しぬ
(die)

5. このは
(leaf)

6. へた
(clumsy)

Ⅲ) Write the words below in *hiragana*.

1. *fune*
(boat)

2. *hoshi*
(star)

3. *hana*
(flower)

4. *heso*
(navel)

5. *nuno*
(cloth)

6. *hiniku*
(sarcasm)

第1課 4 Hiragana (ま – よ)
だい いっ か

Ⅰ Practice writing the following eight *hiragana* (ま through よ).

ma	ま	一 ニ ／ ま	ま	ま	ま				
mi	み	ス み	み	み	み				
mu	む	＼ む ／ む	む	む	む				
me	め	＼ ／ め	め	め	め				
mo	も	し も ／ も	も	も	も				
ya	や	つ ／ や ／ つ	や	や	や				
yu	ゆ	ワ ／ ゆ	ゆ	ゆ	ゆ				
yo	よ	ー ／ よ	よ	よ	よ				

Ⅱ Copy and romanize the words below.

1. まち
   (town)

2. みせ
   (store)

3. むね
   (chest)

4. ゆめ
   (dream)

5. もや
   (fog)

6. よむ
   (read)

Ⅲ Write the words below in *hiragana*.

1. *mochi*
   (rice cake)

2. *matsu*
   (wait)

3. *kami*
   (paper; hair)

4. *oyu*
   (hot water)

5. *musume*
   (daughter)

6. *yoyaku*
   (reservation)

第1課 5 Hiragana (ら – ん)
だい いっ か

Ⅰ Practice writing the following eight *hiragana* (ら through ん).

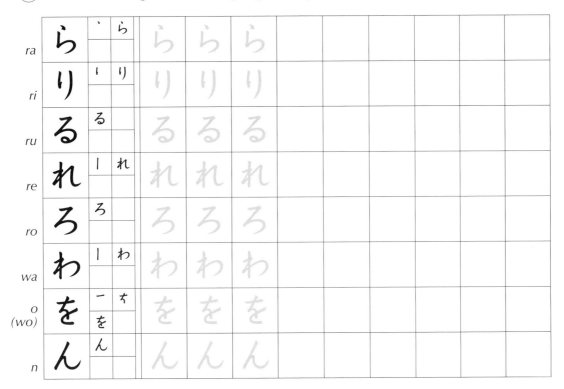

Ⅱ Copy and romanize the words below.

1. わらう
(laugh)

2. よる
(night)

3. きいろ
(yellow)

4. はれ
(sunny)

5. きをつけて
(Watch out!)

6. しんり
(psychology)

Ⅲ Write the words below in *hiragana*.

1. *wakaru*
(understand)

2. *rekishi*
(history)

3. *me o(=wo) samasu*
(wake up)

4. *riron*
(theory)

5. *rainen*
(next year)

6. *han ei*
(prosperity)

第1課 6 Hiragana (Dots/Circles/Small や, ゆ, よ)
だい いっ か

Ⓘ Copy and romanize the words below, paying special attention to letters with dots and circles.

1. できごと
(event)

2. じだい
(historical period)

3. がんばる
(try hard)

4. ばんぱく
(Expo)

Ⓘ Write the words below in *hiragana*, paying attention to letters with dots and circles.

1. *kaba*
(hippo)

2. *gaikokujin*
(foreigner)

3. *mondai*
(problem)

4. *shinpai*
(worry)

Ⓘ Copy and romanize the words below, paying special attention to small *hiragana*.

1. おきゃくさん
(guest)

2. きょねん
(last year)

3. しゃかい
(society)

4. みんしゅしゅぎ
(democracy)

5. おちゃ
(tea)

6. ひゃくえん
(100 yen)

7. きんじょ
(neighborhood)

8. りょかん
(Japanese inn)

Ⓘ Write the words below in *hiragana*, paying special attention to small *hiragana*.

1. *kyoka*
(permission)

2. *densha*
(train)

3. *jinja*
(shrine)

4. *chokin*
(savings)

5. *shukudai*
(homework)

6. *sanbyaku*
(three hundreds)

第1課 7 Hiragana (Double Consonants/Long Vowels)
だい いっ か

(I) Copy and romanize the words below, paying special attention to the double consonants.

1. いっかい
(once)

2. きっさてん
(coffee shop)

3. ずっと
(all along)

4. しっぽ
(tail)

5. あんない
(guide)

(II) Write the words below in *hiragana*, paying attention to the double consonants.

1. *issho*
(together)

2. *motto*
(more)

3. *kippu*
(ticket)

4. *zannen*
(regrettable)

(III) Copy and romanize the words below, paying attention to the long vowels.

1. おかあさん
(mother)

2. おにいさん
(older brother)

3. くうき
(air)

4. へいわ
(peace)

5. そうだん
(consultation)

6. すうじ
(number)

(IV) Write the words below in *hiragana*, paying attention to the long vowels. Note especially that "*ee*" and "*oo*" sequences are transcribed as if they are "*ei*" and "*ou*," respectively.

1. *ojiisan*
(grandfather)

2. *obaasan*
(grandmother)

3. *tsuuyaku*
(interpreter)

4. *gakusee*
(student)

5. *otoosan*
(father)

6. *tookyoo*
(Tokyo)

第2課 1 Katakana (ア – コ)
だい に か

I Practice writing the following ten *katakana* (ア through コ).

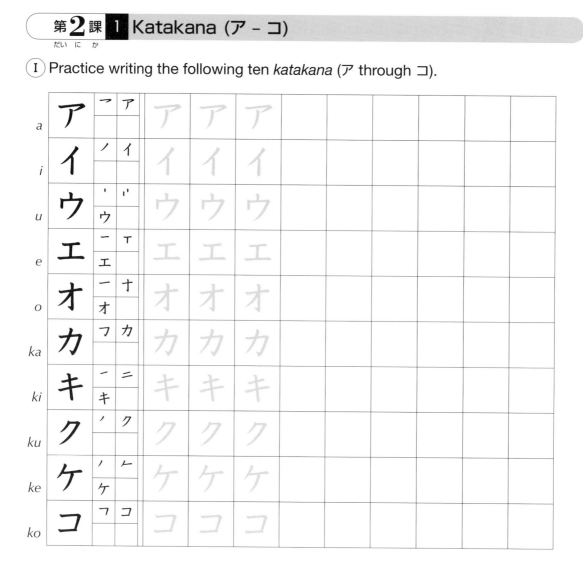

II Write the words below in *katakana*.

Unlike the *hiragana* writing system, long vowels in *katakana* words are transcribed with a bar. For example: リー (りい in *hiragana*), カー (かあ in *hiragana*).

1. おーけー
   (okay)

2. けーき
   (cake)

3. うえあ
   (wear)

4. こーく
   (coke)

5. きうい
   (kiwifruit)

6. ここあ
   (cocoa)

第2課 2 Katakana (サ – ト)
だい　に　か

(I) Practice writing the following ten *katakana* (サ through ト).

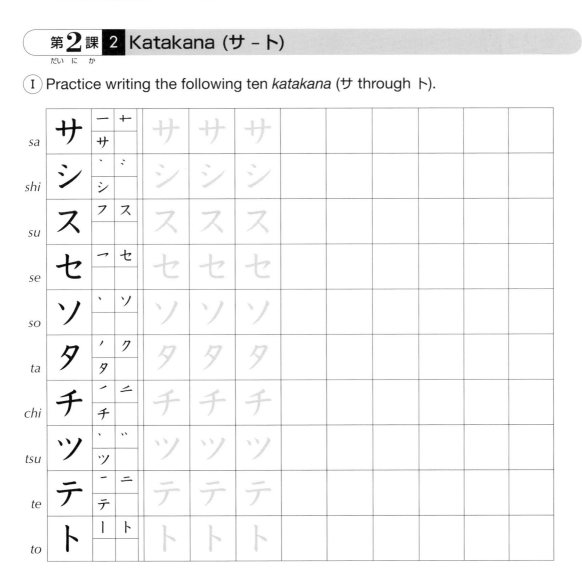

(II) Write the words below in *katakana*.

1. しーざー
   (Caesar)

2. すーつ
   (suit)

3. せっと
   (set)

4. そっくす
   (socks)

5. たこす
   (tacos)

6. ちーず
   (cheese)

7. たい
   (Thailand)

8. でっき
   (deck)

第2課 3 Katakana (ナ – ホ)
だい に か

Ⅰ Practice writing the following ten *katakana* (ナ through ホ).

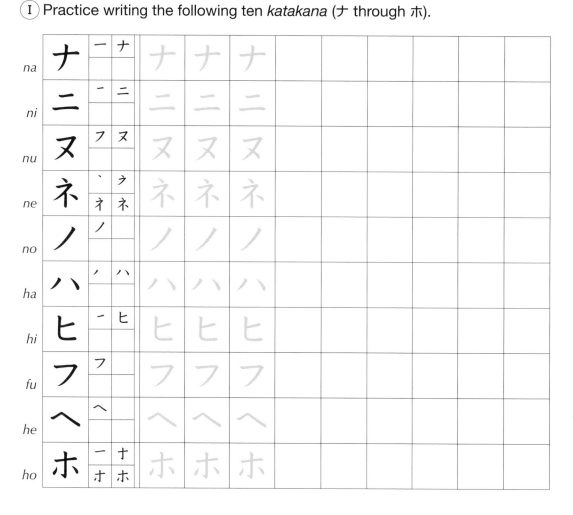

Ⅱ Write the words below in *katakana*.

1. ぼさのば
   (bossa nova)

2. かぬー
   (canoe)

3. はーぶ
   (herb)

4. びきに
   (bikinis)

5. なっつ
   (nuts)

6. ぺっと
   (pet)

7. こね
   (connection)

8. はっぴー
   (happy)

9. ねくたい
   (necktie)

10. のーと
    (notebook)

第2課 4 Katakana (マ – ヨ)
だい に か

Ⅰ Practice writing the following eight *katakana* (マ through ヨ).

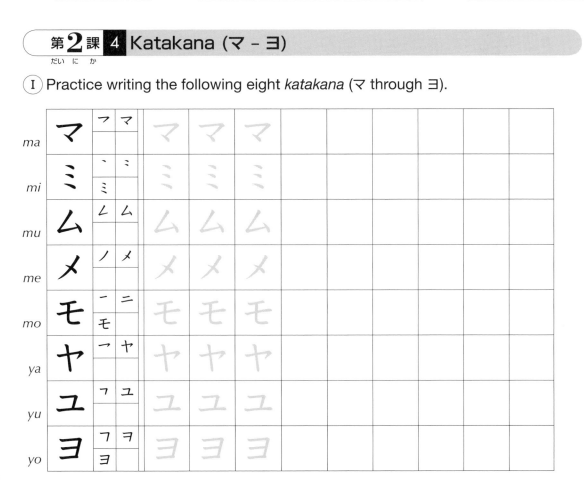

Ⅱ Write the words below in *katakana*.

1. めも
(memo)

2. むーど
(mood)

3. みに
(mini)

4. まや
(Maya)

5. よっと
(yacht)

6. ゆーざー
(user)

7. きゃっぷ
(cap)

8. しちゅー
(stew)

9. しょっく
(shock)

10. はーもにか
(harmonica)

第2課 だいにか 5 Katakana (ラ – ン)

(I) Practice writing the following eight *katakana* (ラ through ン).

ra	ラ	¯ / ラ	ラ	ラ	ラ					
ri	リ	¹ / リ	リ	リ	リ					
ru	ル	ノ / ル	ル	ル	ル					
re	レ	レ	レ	レ	レ					
ro	ロ	¹ ロ / ロ	ロ	ロ	ロ					
wa	ワ	¹ / ワ	ワ	ワ	ワ					
o (wo)	ヲ	¯ = / ヲ	ヲ	ヲ	ヲ					
n	ン	` / ン	ン	ン	ン					

(II) Write the words below in *katakana*.

The small *katakana* エ is used with シ and チ to transcribe the sounds "she" and "che": シェパード (shepherd) and チェック (check), for example.

1. よーろっぱ
   (Europe)

2. わっくす
   (wax)

3. るーれっと
   (roulette)

4. あふりか
   (Africa)

5. らーめん
   (ramen noodle)

6. しぇーくすぴあ
   (Shakespeare)

7. ちぇ・げばら
   (Che Guevara)

8. よーぐると
   (yoghurt)

第3課 1 Kanji Practice

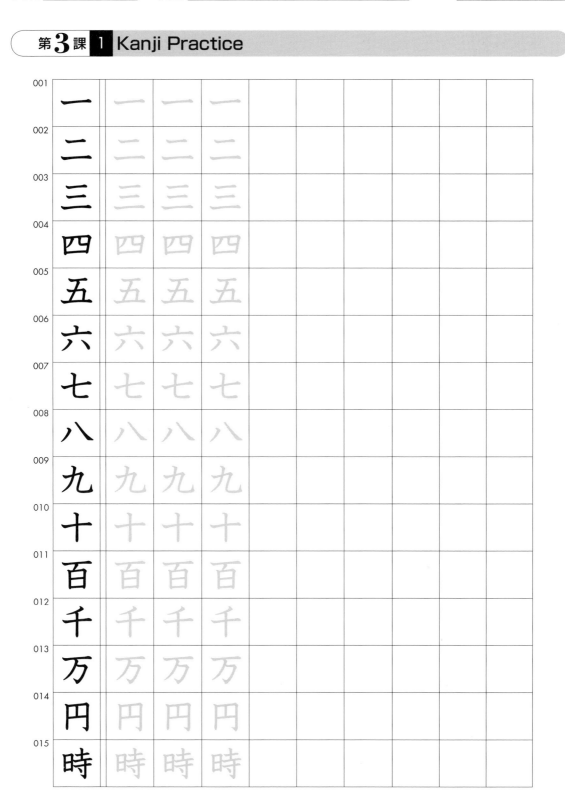

第3課 2 Using Kanji

Ⅰ Write the numbers in kanji.

1. 41

2. 300

3. 1,500

4. 2,890

5. 67,000

6. 128,000

7. 1,000,000

Ⅱ Write in kanji.

1. A：これはいくらですか。　　B：_____です。
　　　　　　　　　　　　　　　　　　　ろっぴゃくえん

2. A：いまなん_____ですか。　B：_____です。
　　　　　　　　じ　　　　　　　　　　じゅうにじ

Ⅲ Using the kanji you know, translate the sentences into Japanese.

1. This watch is 49,000 yen.

2. That bag is 5,300 yen.

3. Ms. Yamanaka gets up at six.

4. Ms. Kawaguchi goes to college at seven.

5. Mr. Suzuki usually goes to bed at about twelve.

6. I sometimes drink coffee at a cafe. The coffee is 180 yen.

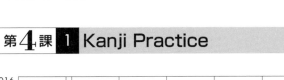

第4課 1 Kanji Practice

016 日	日	日	日					
017 本	本	本	本					
018 人	人	人	人					
019 月	月	月	月					
020 火	火	火	火					
021 水	水	水	水					
022 木	木	木	木					
023 金	金	金	金					
024 土	土	土	土					
025 曜	曜	曜	曜					
026 上	上	上	上					
027 下	下	下	下					
028 中	中	中	中					
029 半	半	半	半					

第4課 2 Using Kanji

Ⓘ Write in kanji.

1. Sunday   5. Thursday

2. Monday   6. Friday

3. Tuesday   7. Saturday

4. Wednesday

Ⓘ Write in kanji.

1. _____ごの_____はかばんの_____です。   2. _____をのみます。
    にほん   ほん   なか   みず

3. いま、_____です。   4. あの_____はだれですか。
        ろくじはん   ひと

5. エレベーター (elevator) は_____にいきますか。_____にいきますか。
                        うえ   した

6. わたしのともだちは_____です。
                    にほんじん

Ⓘ Using the kanji you know, translate the sentences into Japanese.

1. I went to a restaurant with a Japanese friend on Friday.

2. I got up at about ten thirty on Saturday.

3. I went to a temple alone on Monday.

4. The book is on the desk. The newspaper is under the book.

第5課 1 Kanji Practice

030 山	山	山	山						
031 川	川	川	川						
032 元	元	元	元						
033 気	気	気	気						
034 天	天	天	天						
035 私	私	私	私						
036 今	今	今	今						
037 田	田	田	田						
038 女	女	女	女						
039 男	男	男	男						
040 見	見	見	見						
041 行	行	行	行						
042 食	食	食	食						
043 飲	飲	飲	飲						

第5課 2 Using Kanji

Ⓘ Write the appropriate mixes of kanji and *hiragana*.

1. _____ですか。
   げんき

2. _____はいい_____ですね。
   きょう　　　　　　　てんき

3. あの_____の_____は_____さんです。
   おとこ　　ひと　　　やまかわ

4. あの_____の_____は_____さんです。
   おんな　　ひと　　　やまだ

5. _____はきのうレストランに_____。
   わたし　　　　　　　　　　　　　　　いきました

6. ピザを_____。 コーヒーを_____。
   　　　たべました　　　　　　　　　　　　のみました

7. うちでテレビを_____。
   　　　　　　　みました

Ⓘ Using the kanji you know, translate the sentences into Japanese.

1. I am now in Japan.

2. Ms. Tanaka is fine. Mr. Yamakawa is not fine.

3. I went to the mountain with a Japanese man and woman.

4. I drank coffee with my friend on Tuesday.

5. On Wednesday, I ate dinner at home. And then I watched TV.

第6課 1 Kanji Practice

044 東	東	東	東					
045 西	西	西	西					
046 南	南	南	南					
047 北	北	北	北					
048 口	口	口	口					
049 出	出	出	出					
050 右	右	右	右					
051 左	左	左	左					
052 分	分	分	分					
053 先	先	先	先					
054 生	生	生	生					
055 大	大	大	大					
056 学	学	学	学					
057 外	外	外	外					
058 国	国	国	国					

第6課 2 Using Kanji

（I）Write the appropriate mixes of kanji and *hiragana*.

1. _____ _____ _____ _____
   ひがし　にし　みなみ　きた

2. _____を_____、_____へ_____行ってください。
   みなみぐち　　でて　　　みぎ　　ごふん

3. _____を_____、_____へ_____行ってください。
   にしぐち　　　でて　　ひだり　じゅっぷん

4. 山下さんは_____です。
   　　　　　だいがくせい

5. _____はよく_____に行きます。
   せんせい　　　　がいこく

（II）Using the kanji you know, translate the sentences into Japanese.

1. There are lots of foreign teachers in my college.

2. The college is to the left of a bank.

3. Go out the east exit and go to the right, please.

4. The restaurant is near the south exit.

5. I ate fish and drank tea at the restaurant.

6. I waited for twenty minutes at the north exit.

第7課 1 Kanji Practice

059	京	京	京	京						
060	子	子	子	子						
061	小	小	小	小						
062	会	会	会	会						
063	社	社	社	社						
064	父	父	父	父						
065	母	母	母	母						
066	高	高	高	高						
067	校	校	校	校						
068	毎	毎	毎	毎						
069	語	語	語	語						
070	文	文	文	文						
071	帰	帰	帰	帰						
072	入	入	入	入						

第7課 2 Using Kanji

Ⅰ Write the appropriate mixes of kanji and *hiragana*.

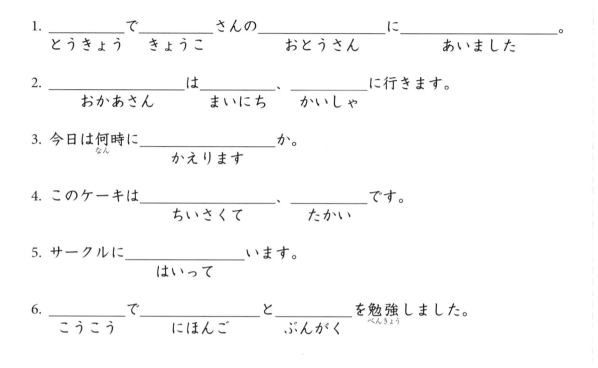

1. _____で_____さんの_____に_____。
   とうきょう　　きょうこ　　　　　　おとうさん　　　　　　あいました

2. _____は_____、_____に行きます。
   おかあさん　　　　　まいにち　　かいしゃ

3. 今日は何時に_____か。
   　　なん　　　　　かえります

4. このケーキは_____、_____です。
   　　　　　ちいさくて　　　　たかい

5. サークルに_____います。
   　　　　　はいって

6. _____で_____と_____を勉強しました。
   こうこう　　　　にほんご　　　　ぶんがく　　べんきょう

Ⅱ Using the kanji you know, translate the sentences into Japanese.

1. Kyoko's younger sister is a high school student.

2. Kyoko's mother works for a small company.

3. Kyoko's father comes home late every day.

4. I am studying Japanese and literature.

5. Ms. Minami speaks English a little.

第8課 1 Kanji Practice

073 員	員	員	員						
074 新	新	新	新						
075 聞	聞	聞	聞						
076 作	作	作	作						
077 仕	仕	仕	仕						
078 事	事	事	事						
079 電	電	電	電						
080 車	車	車	車						
081 休	休	休	休						
082 言	言	言	言						
083 読	読	読	読						
084 思	思	思	思						
085 次	次	次	次						
086 何	何	何	何						

第8課 2 Using Kanji

Ⅰ Write the appropriate mixes of kanji and *hiragana*.

1. 川口さんは_____だと_____。
   かわぐち   かいしゃいん   おもいます

2. 友だちは_____を_____と_____いました。
   とも   しごと   やすむ   いって

3. _____を_____。
   しんぶん   よみます

4. _____ _____を買いました。
   あたらしい   くるま   か

5. ____の_____は_____ですか。
   つぎ   でんしゃ   なんじ

6. _____の日にピザを_____。
   やすみ   つくりました

Ⅱ Using the kanji you know, translate the sentences into Japanese.

1. I read a newspaper on a train.

2. I made a questionnaire.

3. I think company employees in Japan are busy.

4. What do you do on holidays?

5. My mother said that she would go to Tokyo next week.

6. The next train comes at eleven o'clock.

第9課 1 Kanji Practice

087	午	午	午	午						
088	後	後	後	後						
089	前	前	前	前						
090	名	名	名	名						
091	白	白	白	白						
092	雨	雨	雨	雨						
093	書	書	書	書						
094	友	友	友	友						
095	間	間	間	間						
096	家	家	家	家						
097	話	話	話	話						
098	少	少	少	少						
099	古	古	古	古						
100	知	知	知	知						
101	来	来	来	来						

第9課 2 Using Kanji

Ⅰ Write the appropriate mixes of kanji and *hiragana*.

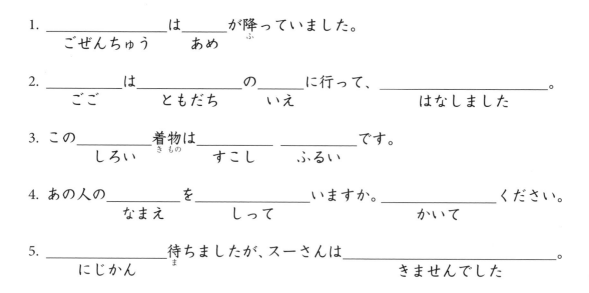

1. _____は_____が降っていました。
      ごぜんちゅう   あめ   ふ

2. _____は_____の_____に行って、_____。
      ごご   ともだち   いえ   はなしました

3. この_____着物は_____ _____です。
      しろい   きもの   すこし   ふるい

4. あの人の_____を_____いますか。_____ください。
       なまえ   しって   かいて

5. _____待ちましたが、スーさんは_____。
      にじかん   ま   きませんでした

Ⅱ Using the kanji you know, translate the sentences into Japanese.

1. I wrote a letter to my friend in the afternoon.

2. I read a book for one hour at home.

3. I had a talk with Ken's father. It was interesting.

4. The name of Mr. Yamashita's dog is Hachi.

5. My dictionary is a little old.

6. Please come to my house. Let's talk.

第**10**課 **1** Kanji Practice

102 住	住	住	住				
103 正	正	正	正				
104 年	年	年	年				
105 売	売	売	売				
106 買	買	買	買				
107 町	町	町	町				
108 長	長	長	長				
109 道	道	道	道				
110 雪	雪	雪	雪				
111 立	立	立	立				
112 自	自	自	自				
113 夜	夜	夜	夜				
114 朝	朝	朝	朝				
115 持	持	持	持				

第10課 2 Using Kanji

Ⅰ) Write the appropriate mixes of kanji and *hiragana*.

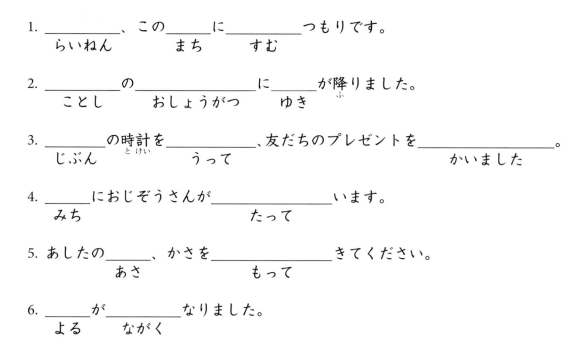

1. _____、この_____に_____つもりです。
   らいねん　　　　　まち　　　すむ

2. _____の_____に_____が降りました。
   ことし　　　　おしょうがつ　　　ゆき　　　　ふ

3. _____の時計を_____、友だちのプレゼントを_____。
   じぶん　　とけい　　　うって　　　　　　　　　　　　　かいました

4. _____におじぞうさんが_____います。
   みち　　　　　　　　　たって

5. あしたの_____、かさを_____きてください。
   あさ　　　　　　もって

6. _____が_____なりました。
   よる　　ながく

Ⅱ) Using the kanji you know, translate the sentences into Japanese.

1. I live in a small town.

2. It snowed yesterday morning.

3. I sold my old car and bought a new one.

4. Ms. Yamada is tall and has long hair.

5. Do you have an umbrella?

6. This road becomes quiet at night.

第11課 1 Kanji Practice

手	手	手	手						
紙	紙	紙	紙						
好	好	好	好						
近	近	近	近						
明	明	明	明						
病	病	病	病						
院	院	院	院						
映	映	映	映						
画	画	画	画						
歌	歌	歌	歌						
市	市	市	市						
所	所	所	所						
勉	勉	勉	勉						
強	強	強	強						
有	有	有	有						
旅	旅	旅	旅						

第11課 2 Using Kanji

Ⅰ Write the appropriate mixes of kanji and *hiragana*.

1. 友だちから_____をもらいました。とても_____人です。
　　　　　　　　　てがみ　　　　　　　　　　　　　　　　　あかるい

2. _____を見たり、_____して、日本語を_____します。
　　　えいが　　　　　　　　うたったり　　　　　　　　　べんきょう

3. 家の_____に_____があります。
　　　ちかく　　　びょういん

4. 父は_____が_____です。
　　　りょこう　　　すき

5. 鎌倉_____に住んでいます。とても_____な_____です。
　　かまくら　し　　　　　　　　　　　　　　ゆうめい　　ところ

Ⅱ Using the kanji you know, translate the sentences into Japanese.

1. On my days off I watch movies, sing songs, and so on.

2. My friend lives in my neighborhood.

3. I traveled to various places.

4. I don't want to go to a hospital tomorrow.

5. I want to become famous in the future.

6. Please write a letter to me.

7. I have never studied foreign languages.

第12課 1 Kanji Practice

132 昔	昔	昔	昔						
133 々	々	々	々						
134 神	神	神	神						
135 早	早	早	早						
136 起	起	起	起						
137 牛	牛	牛	牛						
138 使	使	使	使						
139 働	働	働	働						
140 連	連	連	連						
141 別	別	別	別						
142 度	度	度	度						
143 赤	赤	赤	赤						
144 青	青	青	青						
145 色	色	色	色						

第12課 2 Using Kanji

Ⓘ Write the appropriate mixes of kanji and *hiragana*.

1. _____、ある所に_____がいました。
   むかしむかし   かみさま

2. _____を_____、_____います。
   うし   つかって   はたらいて

3. 毎日、朝_____、_____。
          はやく   おきます

4. 大人は_____ _____、子どもは_____ _____のＴシャツを着ています。
   おとな あかい   いろ   あおい   いろ   ティー   き

5. _____の休みに、友だちを_____ _____。
   こんど   つれて   かえります

6. そこで、友だちと_____。
            わかれました

Ⓘ Using the kanji you know, translate the sentences into Japanese.

1. I like red color and blue color.

2. Let's go to see a movie in the near future.

3. I don't like getting up early in the morning.

4. I don't want to separate from you.

5. May I use a telephone?

6. I have to work this weekend.